Children's
Junior
Encyclopedia

- Easy to read encyclopedia for young children

- More than 500 colourful illustrations

PRASHANT

PUBLICATIONS

Published by

PRASHANT PUBLICATIONS

44-R, New Colony,
Gurgaon 122001 (HR)
Ph.: (0124) 4106344, 2326780

This book is a great collection from many sources, and we are very thankful to all the contributors of this book.

First Published in 2008 by
Prashant Publications, Gurgaon
Copyright © 2008 by Prashant Publications

ISBN : 978-81-87057-57-4

Distributed by
bluebird books

***An Imprint of** Sachdeva Publications*
4598/12-B, Ansari Road,
Daryaganj, New Delhi-110002
Tel : +91-11-23277655, 23276646
E-mail : sachdevapublications@yahoo.co.in

Cover & Typeset by
Kingston

Printed at
S.R.K. Graphics, Delhi

Reprint: 2015

Price : ₹ 375.00

Book One

Space

Book Two

Earth

Book Three
Plants

Book Four
Birds

DISCOVER THE WORLD

THE SPACE

All About Space

Space is all around us. The universe is so enormous, it is impossible to imagine. The universe includes almost everything we can think about, it's very mysterious. All these heavenly bodies like the Sun, Stars, the Moon and our Earth, along with other Planets, are a part of the universe.

▼ **Astronauts** are the people who travel into the space in a space craft.

▼ **Solar Sails** are the spacecrafts without engine, which speeds by the direct pressure of light particles from the Sun. It is the only technology known today that could explore the unlimited boundaries of the outer space in the coming years.

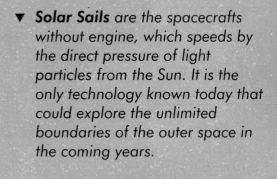

▼ The **'Outer Space'** begins about 200 kms. above the Earth, where the shell of air around our planet disappears. With no air to scatter the sunlight and produce a blue sky, the space appears as a black blanket dotted with stars.

Quiz time!

1. How far have spacecrafts from Earth travelled into space?

2. Which space station is known as the *City in Space*?

3. How fast does the sun travel around the centre of the galaxy?

Answers: 1. *Less than one light day* **2.** *International Space Station* **3.** *150 miles/s.*

Quasars *are the most distant objects in the space.*

*A **Light Year** is the distance travelled by light in one year that is—9.46 million kms.*

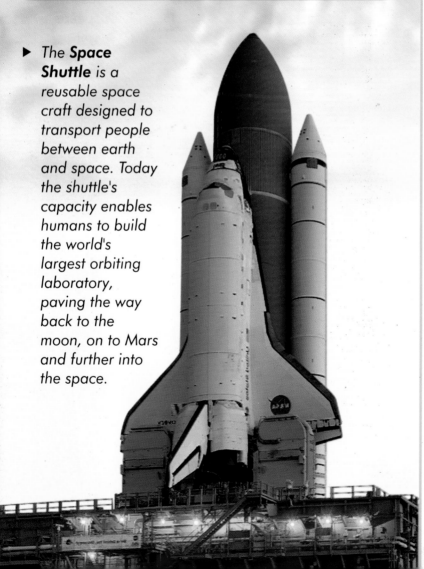

▶ The **Space Shuttle** is a reusable space craft designed to transport people between earth and space. Today the shuttle's capacity enables humans to build the world's largest orbiting laboratory, paving the way back to the moon, on to Mars and further into the space.

Weightlessness *is a feeling an individual experience in space, because the Earth's gravity has less effect on us.*

Composition of Space

The space consists of three types of substances: *normal matter, dark matter and dark energy. The normal matter consists of atoms that makes up the stars, planets human beings and every other visible object in the space.*

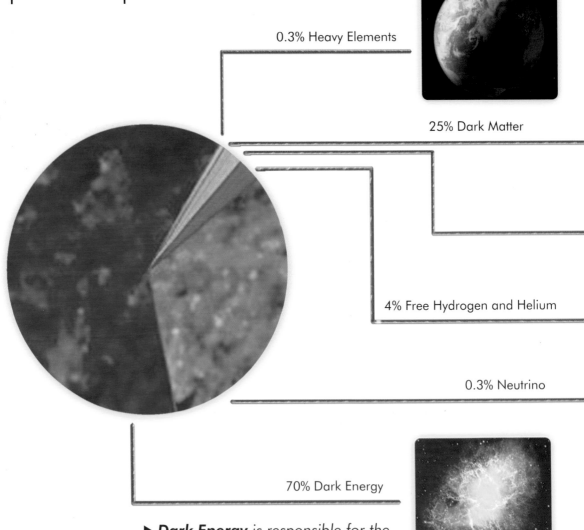

0.3% Heavy Elements

25% Dark Matter

4% Free Hydrogen and Helium

0.3% Neutrino

70% Dark Energy

▶ *Dark Energy is responsible for the expansion of our universe. It constitutes 70% of the space.*

▼ **Dark Matter** that constitutes 25% of the space refers to the matter that does not emit light, and cannot be seen. But its presence can be determined by the gravitational effects on other bodies.

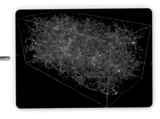

0.6% Stars

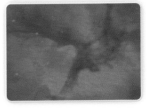

▲ **Hydrogen** and **Helium** are the two most abundant gases in the space.

Space is like a rubber sheet, with a ball in the centre. The more massive the ball, the more curve is the space.

Albert Einstein was the first person to propose the concept of Dark Energy.

Weight of **Galaxies** is measured by measuring the motion of stars.

Galaxies

A galaxy is a huge collection of stars, dust, gas, and other celestial bodies. There are spiral, elliptical, and irregularly shaped galaxies. Individual galaxies are separated by distances in excess of millions of light years. There are believed to be more than one hundred billion galaxies within the total expanse of the universe.

▲ **Milky Way** *is the name of the galaxy, which contain Sun and the nine planets including our Earth. Like all spiral galaxies, it rotates slowly closer to the middle it spins faster than at its edges.*

A typical **Galaxy** contains 10,000,000 to 1,000,000,000,000 stars.

Spiral Galaxies constitute about 80 percent of all galaxies.

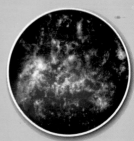

Magellanic Cloud is a dwarf galaxy that is located 160,000 light years away from us.

▲ **Andromeda Galaxy** is the nearest galaxy located 2.9 million light years away, and is the most distant object that can be seen the eye on its own.

Quiz time!

1. What is the size of the Milky Way Galaxy?

2. What is the another name of Andromeda Galaxy?

3. What is the percent of Sefyert Galaxy in our space?

Answers: 1. 100,000 light years in diameter 2. M 31 3. 2%

Stars

A star is a ball of tremendously hot gas, which produces heat and light from nuclear reactions within its core. In a star, the gaseous molecules contain hydrogen and helium, which are bounded by the gravitational force of attraction.

▶ A star generates large amount of energy by the **Nuclear Reaction** in which hydrogen is converted into helium.

Non-burning envelope

Hydrogen-burning shell

Helium-burning shell

Carbon ash

▶ Stars are classified by their **colour**. The hottest, youngest stars are usually yellow, while the coolest and oldest stars are blackish red in colour.

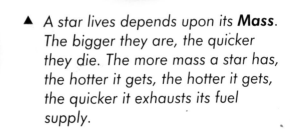

▲ A star lives depends upon its **Mass**. The bigger they are, the quicker they die. The more mass a star has, the hotter it gets, the hotter it gets, the quicker it exhausts its fuel supply.

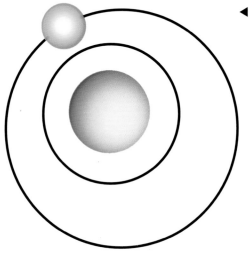

◄ **Binary Star** is a pair of stars which the smaller star orbits around the bigger star, held in place by gravity. Binary Stars are twin in the sense that they are formed together out of the same interstellar cloud.

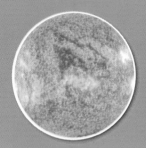

Every second **Sun** emits energy equal to 77 billion megatons.

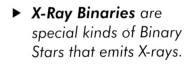 

▶ **X-Ray Binaries** are special kinds of Binary Stars that emits X-rays.

Proxima Centauri is the second nearest star to the Earth after the Sun.

▼ A **Brown Dwarf** is a star whose mass is too small to have nuclear fusion occur at its core. A Brown Dwarf is not a very luminous star.

Super Giants is the largest type of stars, and have short life span of few millions years.

Life and Death of a Star

All stars which are formed in clouds of dust and gas are called the nebulae. The gravitational force causes the denser regions in the nebula to contract into dense clumps. Which grow larger and larger and due to contraction, the temperature inside it rises which finally initiates the nuclear reaction, making the cloud of gases in to a star.

Red Giant Star

▲ A star equal to 1 to 1.5 the size of the Sun ends with the formation of the Red Giant Star.

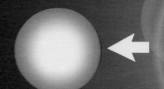

Red Super Giant

▲ A star with mass of 1.5 to 3 times the mass of the Sun became a Red Super Giant after exhausting its fuel.

Main Sequence Star

Star forming the nebula

▼ **Supernova** is the most energetic event in the space. All the stars in our galaxy would have to shine for six months to produce the amount of energy released by just one Supernova.

Explosive Outbursts

Supernova

Recycled Chemicals

Black Hole

▲ A star with three times the mass of the Sun is converted into a Black Hole.

Neutron Star/Pulsar

▲ Stars which are 20 times more massive than our Sun forms the Neutron stars.

Interstellar Medium

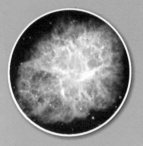

Neutron Stars are about 20 kms. in diameter and weigh 1.5 times more than the Sun.

Pulsars are fast rotating Neutron Stars that emit radio waves.

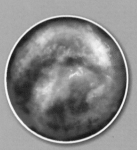

SN 1604 was Supernova observed by Johannes Kepler in 1604.

Supernova

Supernova explosions are the most energetic event in the outer space. These occur at the end of a star's lifetime, when its nuclear fuel is exhausted and it is no longer supported by the release of nuclear energy.

▼ During the **supernova explosion,** a star outshine for months and radiates as much energy as the Sun would emit over about 10 billion years.

◄ The material that is exploded away from the star is now known as a **supernova remnant**.

▼ The **Crab Nebula** is a remnant of a supernova explosion which exploded in 1054.

Supernova explosion occurs about once every 50 years in the **Milky Way Galaxy**.

The supernova explosion was seen by **Johannes Kepler** in 1604.

▼ **Supernova explosion** occurs only in those stars which are 8 times or more massive than our Sun.

Did you Know?

When a star dies in a huge **supernova** explosion, only its dense core may survive.

13

Black Hole

A black hole is a region in space with a strong gravitational field. The gravity of the Black hole is so strong that nothing escapes from it, not even light, the fastest thing in the space. It acts like a giant vaccum cleaner. And anything that gets too close gets sucked in.

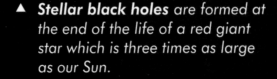

▲ **Stellar black holes** are formed at the end of the life of a red giant star which is three times as large as our Sun.

▶ The concept of black hole was first proposed by **Albert Einstein** in 1915 to explain the theory of general relativity.

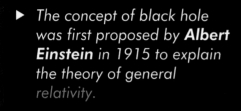

The term black hole was coined by American scientist **John Archibald Wheeler** in 1979.

Black holes can only be detected by **X-ray satellites**.

▲ **Cygnus X-1** is the nearest known black hole in the outer space. It is located about 8000 light years away.

◀ **Sagittarius A** in the centre of Milky Way is probably a massive black hole of about a million solar masses.

Did you Know?

Some scientist think that in the middle of our galaxy lies an enormous black hole, surrounded by a mass of ancient red stars.

Nebula

A nebula is a cloud of gas and dust in outer space. These clouds are often very large, spanning across many light years. The nebula are created by both the formation and destruction of stars. There are many different kinds of nebula in the sky.

▶ *Hourglass Nebula* *situated in the southern constellation, Musca is about 8,000 light-years away from Earth.*

◀ *The **colours** in a bright nebula depends on the types of gases it contains, like oxygen glows green-blue, while hydrogen glows pink or white.*

▶ *A **Ring Nebula** in Lyra which is 2,000 light-years from Earth.*

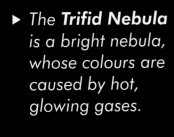

▶ The **Trifid Nebula** is a bright nebula, whose colours are caused by hot, glowing gases.

The **Orion Nebula** is roughly 30 light-years in diameter.

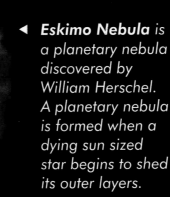

◀ **Eskimo Nebula** is a planetary nebula discovered by William Herschel. A planetary nebula is formed when a dying sun sized star begins to shed its outer layers.

A **Reflection Nebula** glows as the dust in it reflects the light of nearby stars.

Eagle Nebula consists of hydrogen gas and are about 7,000 light-years from Earth.

Quiz time!

1. Which was the last satellite to visit the Venus?

2. How far is the planet, Venus from Sun?

3. How many moons does Venus have?

Answers: 1. Magellan in 1990 2. 67 million miles 3. None

Constellations

The constellations are made up of the most prominent stars in the sky. From the Earth, the stars in a constellation may look quite close to one another, but in reality they are extremely for apart. All constellations can be seen with the naked eye, though what you can see depends on the time of year and the geographical position. Many of them are named after characters taken from the ancient Greek myths.

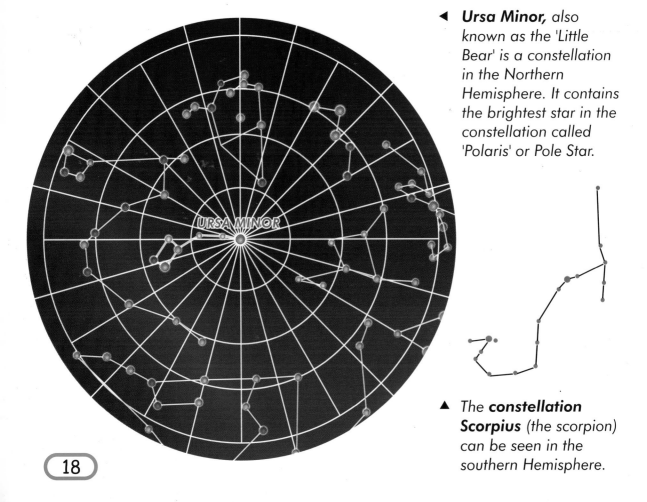

◄ **Ursa Minor,** also known as the 'Little Bear' is a constellation in the Northern Hemisphere. It contains the brightest star in the constellation called 'Polaris' or Pole Star.

▲ The **constellation Scorpius** (the scorpion) can be seen in the southern Hemisphere.

▼ The **Southern Constellations** is a large group of 32 constellations, many of them named during the age of exploration that followed the voyages of Columbus in 1492.

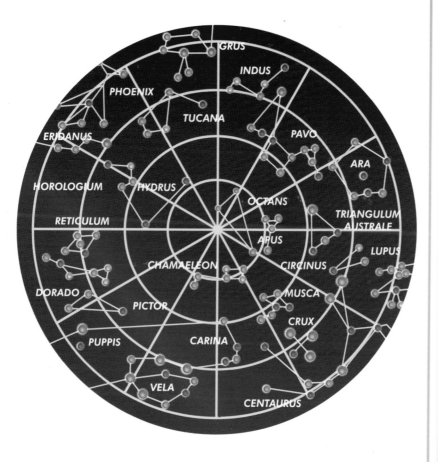

Hydrus is the largest constellation covering 3.15% of the sky.

Crux is the smallest constellation in the night sky.

Cassiopeia is a constellation similar to alphabet 'W' formed by 5 bright stars.

Quiz time!

1. How many constellations are there?

2. How many constellations did Ptolemy list?

3. What constellation represents a unicorn?

4. The "Signs of the Zodiac" refer to how many

Answers: 1. 88 2. 48 3. Monoceros 4. 12

The Solar System

The Solar system is consist of the sun and nine planets and their moons. It is a very big planetary family. Some visitors like comets and asteroids are also part of our family. Most of the bodies in the solar system travel around the Sun along nearly circular paths called orbit. Solar system formation began billions of years ago, when gases and dust began to come together to form the Sun, planets, and other bodies of the solar system.

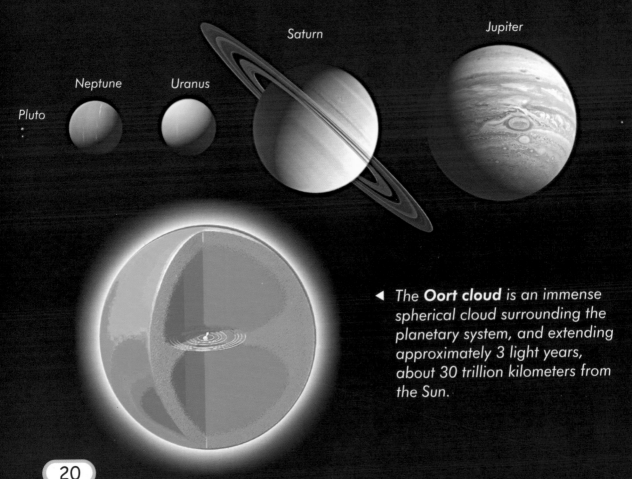

Pluto

Neptune

Uranus

Saturn

Jupiter

◄ The **Oort cloud** is an immense spherical cloud surrounding the planetary system, and extending approximately 3 light years, about 30 trillion kilometers from the Sun.

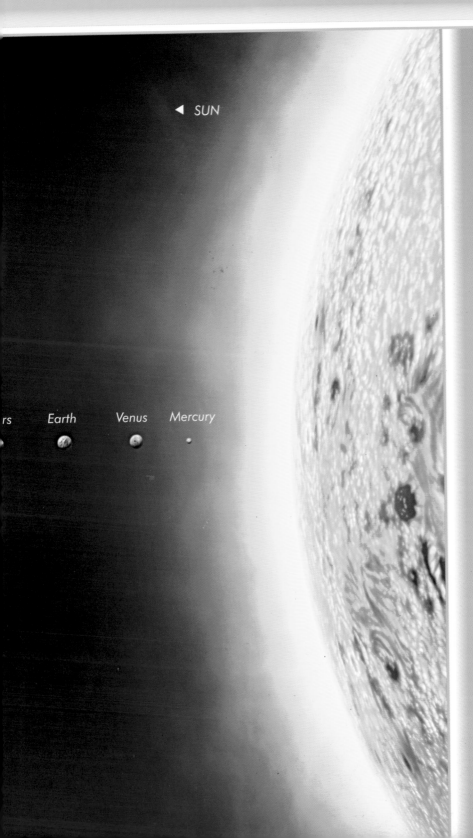

◄ SUN

Earth   Venus   Mercury

rs

Comets are made of ice, dust and rock, and moves around the sun.

Kuiper belt is a ring of ice that circles around the solar system.

Asteroid Belt

Jupiter   Mars

Christiaan Huygens discovered Saturn's rings and its largest moon, Titan in 1655.

The Milky Way

The Milky Way is over 100,000 light-years wide. It is called a spiral galaxy because it has long arms which spin around like a giant pinwheel. Our Sun is a star in one of the arms. When you look up at the night sky, most of the stars you see are in one of the Milky Way arms. Milky Way has three main components: a disk, in which the solar system resides, a central bulge at the core, and an all encompassing halo.

▶ The main disk of the **Milky Way Galaxy** is about 80,000 to 100,000 light-years in diameter

▶ Milky Way is **spiral shaped galaxies** that consist of over 400 billion stars, gases and dust.

▶ Scientists now estimate that in roughly three billion years, the Milky Way galaxy will actually collide with the **Andromeda Galaxy,** which is very slowly working its way towards us at a modest speed of about 1,800 kilometers per minute.

The Milky Way gets its name from a **Greek myth** about the goddess Hera who sprayed milk across the sky.

◀ The Milky Way is believed to be more than **13 billion** years old

From the Earth, our **Milky Way Galaxy** is visible as a milky band that stretches across the night sky.

◀ Our **Sun** is one of these stars and is located roughly 24,000 light years from the center of our the Milky Way.

Did you Know?

The **Sun** revolves around the center of the Milky Way at a speed of half a million miles per hour.

The Sun

The Sun is the largest object in the Solar System. It contains approximately 98% of the total mass of the Solar System mass. The Sun appears to have been active for about 4.6 billion years, and has enough fuel to go on for another 5 billion years or so.

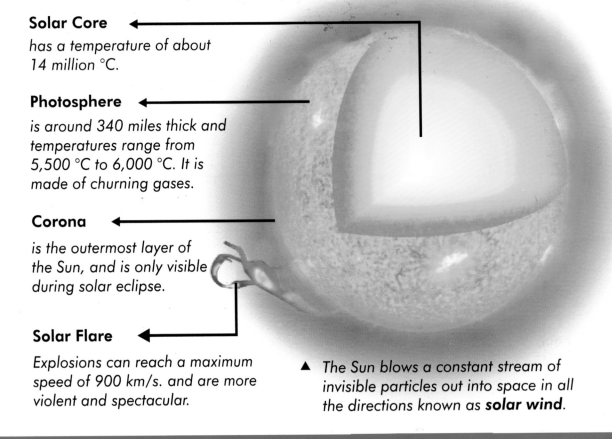

Solar Core

has a temperature of about 14 million °C.

Photosphere

is around 340 miles thick and temperatures range from 5,500 °C to 6,000 °C. It is made of churning gases.

Corona

is the outermost layer of the Sun, and is only visible during solar eclipse.

Solar Flare

Explosions can reach a maximum speed of 900 km/s. and are more violent and spectacular.

▲ *The Sun blows a constant stream of invisible particles out into space in all the directions known as* **solar wind**.

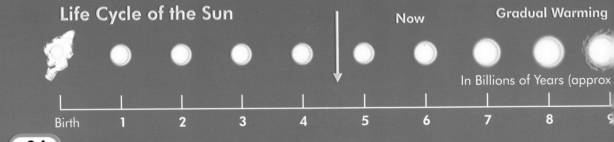

Life Cycle of the Sun

Now

Gradual Warming

In Billions of Years (approx

Birth   1   2   3   4   5   6   7   8   9

▼ The **Solar** and **Heliospheric Observatory** (SOHO) weighs about two tons and with its solar panels extended it stands about 25 feet across. The spacecraft has 12 scientific instruments collecting information about sunspots, the corona, solar flares and vibrations deep in the Sun's interior.

Northern lights are caused due to the interaction between the solar wind and the Earth's atmosphere.

The **Ulysses** is the first spacecraft to explore the poles of the Sun.

▶ A **Sunspot** are a small, dark patches region on the Sun's photosphere that is cooler and darker than the surrounding material.

Red Giant

Planetary Nebula

White Dwarf...

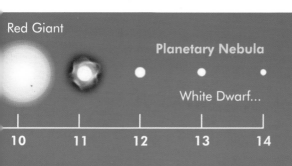

10	11	12	13	14

Did you Know?

The **Sun's diameter** is about 110 times bigger than that of the Earth.

25

Mercury

Mercury is a very small planet, with a diameter of only 4,850 km. and it is the nearest planet to the Sun, orbiting it at a distance of about 58 million km. Due to its closeness, Mercury is blasted by the sun's rays. Its daytime temperature can reach 427°C, which is over four times hotter than boiling water. It takes 88 Earth days to orbit the Sun.

▶ The only visit to Mercury was made by the **Mariner 10** spacecraft in 1974.

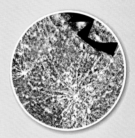

The largest crater is **Beethoven,** about 643 kms in diameter, and is the largest in the Solar System.

Caloris Basin is around 1300 kms in diameter and was probably caused by an impact from an object larger than 100 kms in diameter.

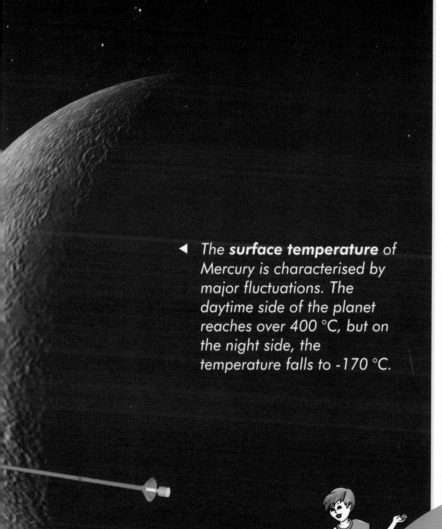

◄ The **surface temperature** of Mercury is characterised by major fluctuations. The daytime side of the planet reaches over 400 °C, but on the night side, the temperature falls to -170 °C.

Did you Know?

Mercury is so close to the Sun, and so small, that it has only a very small atmosphere.

Mercury

Venus

Venus is the hottest and the second planet in the Solar System. The atmosphere of Venus is mainly composed of carbon dioxide and nitrogen, with traces of other gases, and little or no water vapour. Similar in size, density, and mass, Venus and Earth are often referred to as sister planets.

▶ The clouds in **Venus'** atmosphere are composed of sulfuric acid which causes the planet to reflect 65% of the sunlight that reaches it. Thus, Venus is the third brightest object in the sky.

◀ Venus has been visited by over 20 spacecrafts. The first visit was made by **Mariner 2** in 1962.

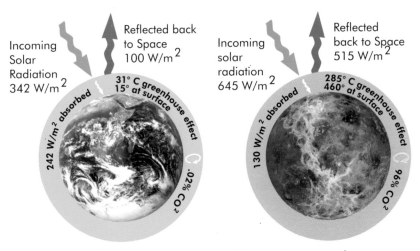

Incoming Solar Radiation 342 W/m^2

Reflected back to Space 100 W/m^2

242 W/m^2 absorbed

31° C greenhouse effect
15° at surface

.02% CO$_2$

Incoming solar radiation 645 W/m^2

Reflected back to Space 515 W/m^2

130 W/m^2 absorbed

285° C greenhouse effect
460° at surface

96% CO$_2$

Sif Mons, a volcano on planet Venus is about 2 kms. high, and about 300 kms. in diameter.

▲ The **surface temperature** of Venus is more than 490 °C. The high temperature of the planet is due to the presence of carbon dioxide that cases the green house effects, and any rays that travel through it becomes trapped.

▶ Venus is the only planet in the Solar System to turn **clockwise**.

*The planet, Venus is named after the Roman God of **Love and Beauty**.*

Quiz time!

1. Which was the last satellite to visit the Venus?

2. How far is the planet, Venus from Sun?

3. How many moons does Venus have?

Answers: 1. Magellan in 1990 2. 67 million miles 3. None

29

The Earth

The Earth is the fifth largest planet in the Solar System. It is the only presently known planet in the Solar System to support life. The Earth is around 4.6 billion years old.

▶ The Earth is composed of three layers: a **core**, a **mantle**, and an outer **crust**. Core is the innermost layer, and is about 2,600 kms. thick. The middle layer, which is about the 2,900 kms. thick is Mantle. Crust is the outermost thinnest layer measuring only 8 to 10 kms. in thickness.

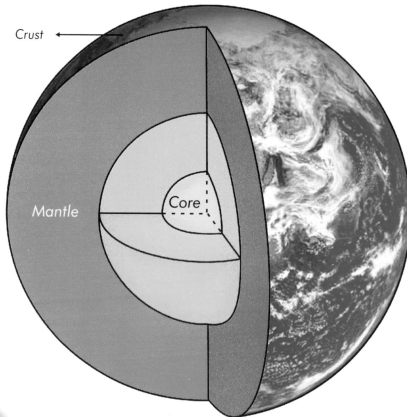

Crust

Mantle

Core

▲ Earth's inner core is a hot ball of solid iron. It is surrounded by a layer of liquid iron, then a thick, rocky mantel. The uttermost layer is a thin rocky shell known as the crust.

◀ The Earth has only one natural satellite, the **Moon**. The Moon is the second brightest object in the sky.

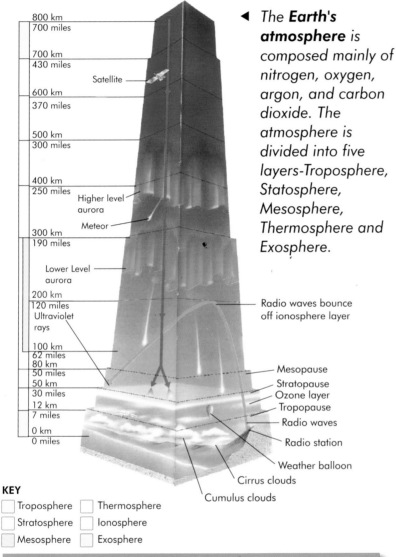

800 km
700 miles

700 km
430 miles

Satellite

600 km
370 miles

500 km
300 miles

400 km
250 miles

Higher level aurora

Meteor

300 km
190 miles

Lower Level aurora

200 km
120 miles
Ultraviolet rays

100 km
62 miles
80 km
50 miles
50 km
30 miles
12 km
7 miles

0 km
0 miles

Mesopause
Stratopause
Ozone layer
Tropopause
Radio waves
Radio station
Weather balloon
Cirrus clouds
Cumulus clouds

Radio waves bounce off ionosphere layer

◀ The **Earth's atmosphere** is composed mainly of nitrogen, oxygen, argon, and carbon dioxide. The atmosphere is divided into five layers-Troposphere, Statosphere, Mesosphere, Thermosphere and Exosphere.

KEY

☐ Troposphere	☐ Thermosphere
☐ Stratosphere	☐ Ionosphere
☐ Mesosphere	☐ Exosphere

The **Mount Everest** in the Himalayas, is the tallest mountain on Earth.

Located in Africa, the **Sahara**, is the largest desert on Earth.

The **Grand Canyon** stretches over 350 kms of land and is formed by the Colorado River.

Quiz time!

1. Which is the most abundant gas in the atmosphere?

2. Which layer of atmosphere protect us from the harmful ultraviolet rays of Sun?

3. What elements are found in the core of the Earth?

Answers: 1. Nitrogen 2. Ozone Layer 3. Iron and Nickle

Mars

Mars is the fourth planet from the Sun and the seventh largest in the Solar System. It is commonly referred to as the Red Planet because of the reddish dust covering its surface. Mars takes about 12 earth years to complete one orbit around the Sun.

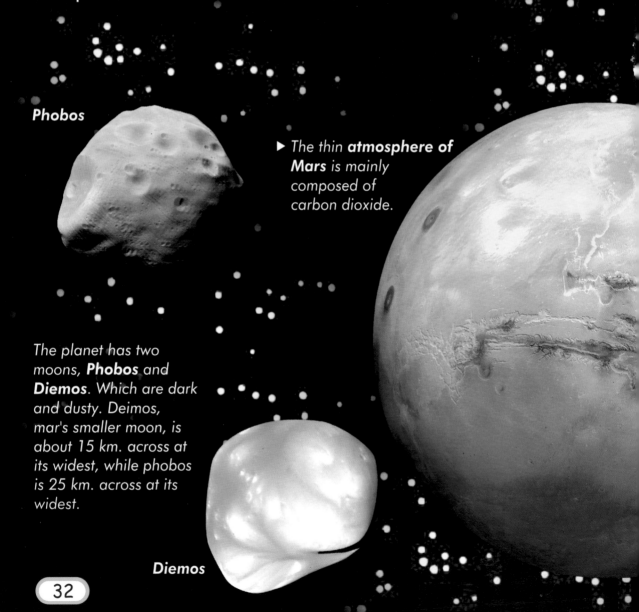

Phobos

▶ The thin **atmosphere of Mars** is mainly composed of carbon dioxide.

The planet has two moons, **Phobos** and **Diemos**. Which are dark and dusty. Deimos, mar's smaller moon, is about 15 km. across at its widest, while phobos is 25 km. across at its widest.

Diemos

▼ Mars was first visited by the **Mariner 4**, in 1965, which transmitted 22 pictures of the Martian surface back to Earth.

The most successful Mars missions, called **Mars pathfinder** and Mars Global surveyor, were launched in 1996.

▼ **Olympus Mons**, a 550 kms wide volcano, is the largest volcano in the solar system. It is around 27 kms high in contrast to Mt Everest on Earth at 8.85 kms.

The Planet Mars is named after The **God of War** in Roman mythology.

Jupiter

Jupiter is the largest planet in the Solar System. Its diameter is more than 11 times the diameter of Earth. Jupiter takes about 12 years to complete one orbit around the Sun and rotates in about 10 hours.

▼ If **Jupiter** had been a little larger, the planet could have started its own nuclear reaction, and become another Sun.

▶ The **Great Red Spot** is a huge storm that has been continuously going on in Jupiter for over 400 years. Winds inside this storm reach speeds of about 270 mph. With a diameter of 15,400 miles, this storm is three times the size of the Earth.

Ganymede is the largest moon in the solar system.

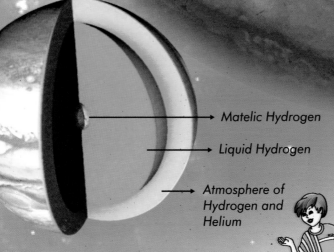

→ Matelic Hydrogen

→ Liquid Hydrogen

→ Atmosphere of Hydrogen and Helium

The **Pioneer 10** was the first spacecraft to visit Jupiter in 1973.

♦ Jupiter is about **90% hydrogen** and **10% helium** with traces of methane, water, and ammonia.

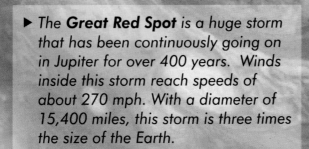

Did you Know?

Like Saturn, Jupiter has **rings**, though they are much smaller fainter, and darker.

Saturn

Saturn is a giant gas planet and the second largest in the Solar System after Jupiter. The planet is known for its prominent ring system. Saturn is flattened at the poles, and budges at the equator because of its very rapid rotation.

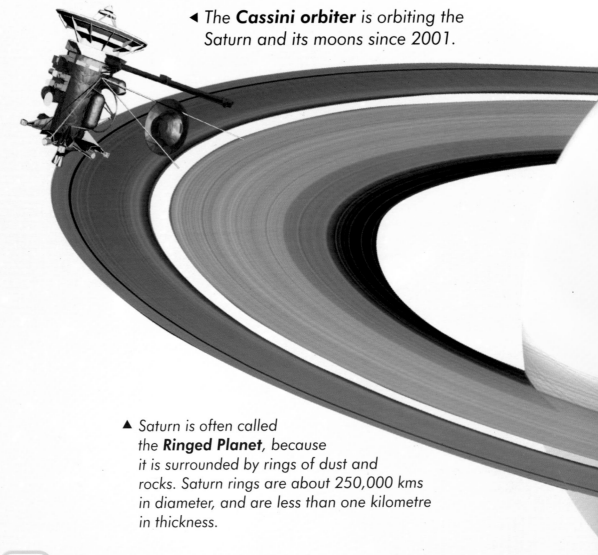

◄ The **Cassini orbiter** is orbiting the Saturn and its moons since 2001.

▲ Saturn is often called the **Ringed Planet**, because it is surrounded by rings of dust and rocks. Saturn rings are about 250,000 kms in diameter, and are less than one kilometre in thickness.

▼ *Saturn is approximately* **75% hydrogen** *and* **25% helium** *with traces of other substances like methane and water ice.*

Titan, *the biggest moon of Saturn is the only moon in the Solar System to have a dense atmosphere.*

Galileo *discovered Saturn in 1610.*

Christiaan Huygens *discovered Saturn's rings and its largest moon, Titan in 1655.*

Uranus

Uranus is the third largest planet in the Solar System. The atmosphere of Uranus is composed of hydrogen, helium, and methane. The methane in the atmosphere absorbs red light, giving the planet a blue-green colour.

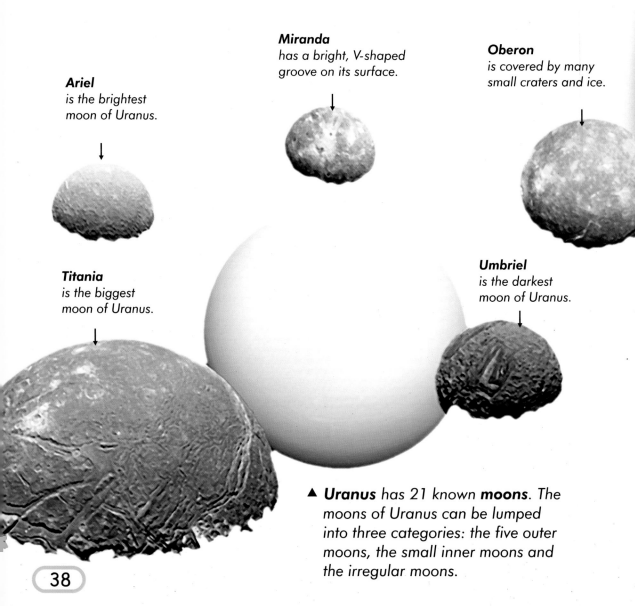

Miranda
has a bright, V-shaped groove on its surface.

Oberon
is covered by many small craters and ice.

Ariel
is the brightest moon of Uranus.

Titania
is the biggest moon of Uranus.

Umbriel
is the darkest moon of Uranus.

▲ **Uranus** *has 21 known* **moons**. *The moons of Uranus can be lumped into three categories: the five outer moons, the small inner moons and the irregular moons.*

Uranus poles actually point towards the Sun.

Uranus was discovered by **William Herschel** in 1781.

Uranus is named after the **Greek God of the sky**.

▲ Uranus has **rings** that are composed of fine dust, rocks, and ice boulders.

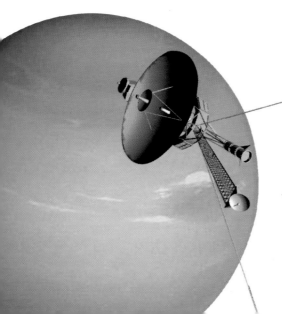

◄ **Voyager 2** is the only spacecraft to have visited Uranus in 1986.

Neptune

Neptune is the fourth largest planet in the Solar System discovered by astronomers John Couch Adams and Urbain Jean Joseph Le Verrier. It is a gas planet, composed of hydrogen, helium, and methane, with traces of ammonia and water. The planet was first discoverd on 23rd september, 1846 by Germon Astronomer Johann Galle using Le Verrieis and J.C. Adam's mathematical predictions.

Layered Atmosphere of hydrogen, helium, and methane

Liquid hydrogen

Mantle icy water, ammoniae, and methane

Core silicate rock

▶ The **blue colour** of the planet is due to the absorption of red light by methane in the atmosphere.

◀ **Triton** is the largest moon of Neptune, and orbits the planet in backwards direction.

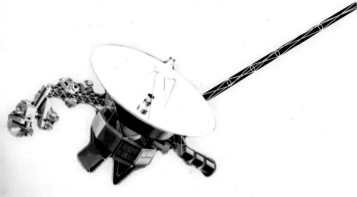

▲ The only spacecraft ever to visit Neptune was the **Voyager 2** in 1989.

Neptune has a four rings which are narrow and very faint and are made of rocks and dust.

▼ Neptune has stronger winds than any other planet in the Solar System. The **Great Dark Spot** winds blow up to 2,000 kilometres an hour.

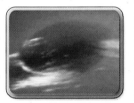

Great Dark Spot

Neptune is the **God of the sea** in Roman Mythology.

Did you Know?

Neptune radiates almost three times of as much heat energy as it gets from the distant Sun.

41

Pluto

Pluto is called a dwarf planet far from the Sun. It is the Solar System's smallest, coldest and most distant object. Pluto is so cold that nitrogen and oxygen, which we breathe so easily on Earth, become frozen solid.

▶ Pluto has a single moon called, **Charon**, which is not much smaller than Pluto itself discovered in 1975. Pluto is about 2,280 kms. wide, while Charon is around 1,212 kms. wide.

◀ **Pluto** is the planet with the lowest pull of gravity in the Solar System. This will explain why its moon, Charon, orbits the planet so closely at a distance of about 19,640 kms.

▶ Pluto has the **largest orbit** around the Sun. It takes almost 248 years to complete one revolution around the Sun. Also its orbit is tilted at an angle compared with other planets. It cuts across Neptune's orbit.

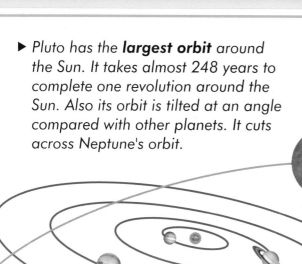

Pluto was discovered in 1930 by **Clyde Tombaugh**, an American astronomers.

▶ Pluto is the only planet in the Solar System not to have been visited by a **space probe**. NASA has planned to send a spacecraft, New Horizon on the planet by 2015.

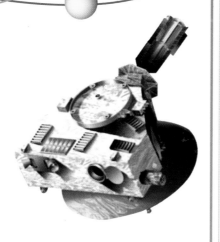

Pluto's volume is about 0.66% that of **Earth's.**

Did you Know?

Ploto is today surrounded by controversy by the scientist, for they are of the opinion it is no longer a part of solar system!

Space Observatory

A space observatory is any instrument in outer space. Used for observation of distant planets, galaxies, and other space objects. Viewing the space from Earth is difficult due to the Earth's atmosphere, so it became necessary to place the space observatory in Earth's orbit.

▶ The **Compton Gamma-Ray Observatory** *studied several phenomena in the universe such as solar flares, quasars and cosmic-ray interactions, before its mission ended in 1999.*

◀ *The **Hubble Space Telescope** is 50 times more sensitive than ground-based telescopes, with 10 times better resolution. Hubble whirls around Earth at 5 miles per second.*

Most was launched In 2003, and is the smallest space telescope in the world.

▲ **Spitzer Space Telescope orbits** around the Sun in trailing Earth in its orbit. The telescope drifts away from us at about 15 million kms. per year.

Herschel Space Observatory is about four times as far away as the moon.

◄ The **James Webb Space Telescope** is intended to replace the Hubble Space Telescope, and is planned for launch no earlier than June 2013.

The Chandra X-Ray Observatory examines phenomena such as supernovas and black holes in outer space.

Space Explorations

Space explorations are the activities that scientists do by sending spacecrafts in outer space to explore the secrets of the universe. Launching of unmanned spacecrafts Sputnik was the first step in space exploration. Since then, we have built space stations, and humans have visited the moon, and most of our Solar System has been visited by robotic explorers.

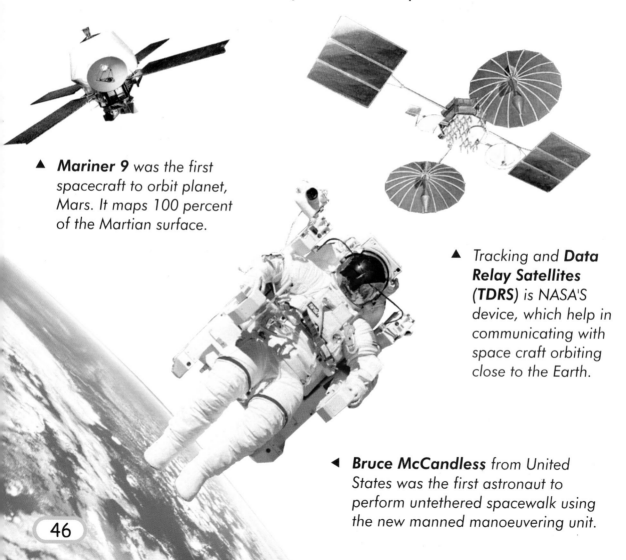

▲ **Mariner 9** was the first spacecraft to orbit planet, Mars. It maps 100 percent of the Martian surface.

▲ Tracking and **Data Relay Satellites (TDRS)** is NASA'S device, which help in communicating with space craft orbiting close to the Earth.

◄ **Bruce McCandless** from United States was the first astronaut to perform untethered spacewalk using the new manned manoeuvering unit.

▶ On Arpril 12, 1981, the first manned mission of the **Space Transportation System (STS-1)**, Columbia, was launched.

▲ The **Satellite Hopparcos** was launched by the European space agency in 1989 For three and a half years, it mapped the night sky in greatest detail.

Sputnik 1 was the world's first artificial satellite weighting at 184 pounds.

◀ **Neil Armstrong, Edwin Aldrin, Jr. and Michael Collins** were the first persons to set foot on moon on July 20, 1969.

Laika was the first animal to be sent into the space.

Russian astronout, **Yuri Gagarin** became the first human to venture into the space.

Quiz time!

1. On which asteroid spacecraft, NEAR was landed?

2. Who was the first tourist to fly into the space?

3. Which was the spacecraft to land on moon?

4. When was NASA born?

Answers: 1. Eros 2. 67 Dennis Tito 3. Luna 9 4. October 1, 1958

Glossary

Dwarf planet: Very small object that moves around the sun.

Exosphere: The outermost, least dense portion of the atmosphere.

Gamma ray: A type of high-energy radiation that is different from an x-ray.

Green house effect: Process in which green house gases, like carbon dioxide in the Earth's atmosphere, cause thermal radiation emitted by the Earth's surface to be reflected back down, therefore causing the climate to warm.

Light years: The distance light travels in one year: roughly 9.46×1012 kilometres (9.46 petametres, or about 5.88×1012 (nearly six trillion) miles).

Manned maneuvering Unit: The manned maneuvering unit is a one-man propulsion backpack that snaps onto the back of the space suit's portable life-support system. The MMU allows the astronaut to work outside without a tether and is able to move as far as 300 feet from the orbiter.

Manned mission: A manned mission is usually in reference to launching a human into orbit or to astronomical destinations, such as planetary bodies or other star systems.

Mesosphere: The atmospheric shell between 20 kms. and about 70 to 80 kms., extending from the top of the stratosphere.

Mythical figure: Having to do with a traditional or legendary story, usually one that contains superhuman beings or magical events. For example, stories about Greek gods like Hercules are mythical stories.

NASA: US Civilian Space Agency created by Congress. founded in 1958.

Northern hemisphere: The half of a planet's surface (or celestial sphere) that is north of the equator.

Observatory: A building designed and equipped to observe astronomical phenomena.

Radio waves: The portion of the electromagnetic spectrum having wavelengths longer than about 10 cm.

Red giant: A giant star whose surface temperature is relatively low, so that it glows with a red colour

Resolution: The ability of a microscope or telescope to measure the angular separation of images that are close together.

Revolution: The movement of a celestial body in an orbit around another celestial body.

Rotation: Rotation is the movement of a body in such a way that the distance between a certain fixed point and any given point of that body remains constant.

Satellite: An object that revolves around a planet.

Southern hemisphere: The part of Earth's surface that is south of the equator.

Spacecraft: A vehicle that travels through space. Spacecraft include robotic or unmanned space probes as well as manned vehicles. The term is sometimes also used to describe artificial satellites, which have similar design criteria.

Space probe: An unmanned research craft sent into space.

Space walk: Any kind of physical activity outside a spacecraft by one of the crew.

Stratosphere: Layer of the atmosphere above the troposphere.

Thermosphere: Outermost layer of the atmosphere, above the mesosphere.

Troposphere: The lowest layer of the atmosphere and contains about 95 percent of the mass of air in the Earth's atmosphere.

Weightlessness: The experience during freefall.

White dwarf: A small, hot star near the end of its nuclear fusion period.

X-ray: A type of radiation of very short wavelength and very high energy; x-rays have shorter wavelengths than ultraviolet light but longer wavelengths than cosmic rays.

DISCOVER THE WORLD

THE EARTH

Earth

Earth is the third planet in the Solar System in terms of distance from the Sun. It is the only place in the universe known to human beings to support life. Unlike the other planets, the Earth has a unique set of characteristics ideally suited for supporting life.

▼ The **Earth** was formed around 4.5 billion years ago, and it has been constantly changing and developing ever since.

Rotation

◄ Earth has a **total surface** area of about 196,800,00 square miles. The land consists of only about 29% of the total area while 71% of the total surface area is covered with water.

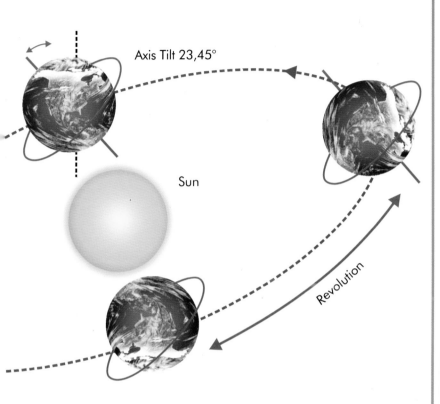

Axis Tilt 23,45°

Sun

Revolution

▲ The Earth completes one **rotation** in 24 hours which makes day and night. The Earth revolves around the Sun and completes one **revolution** in about 365 days which makes one year.

Like a magnet, the Earth also has a **magnetic field**.

The **Moon** is the only natural satellite of the planet, Earth.

The **Sun's rays** take 8 minutes and 20 seconds to reach the Earth.

Quiz time!

1. Which continent is the smallest?

2. What is the name of the world's biggest desert?

3. What is the name of the earth's largest freshwater lake?

4. Which waterfall is the highest?

Answers: 1. Australia **2.** Sahara Desert **3.** Lake Baykal 9 **4.** Angle Falls

Earth's Structure

Ever wondered what our Earth is made of? Think of it as an apple. An apple constitutes the skin, the pulp and the core in the middle. Similarly, the Earth is made up of the thin outermost layer called the crust, the innermost part called the *core*, and the part in between them called the *mantle*. All the layers are pulled by the enormous force of gravity from the centre.

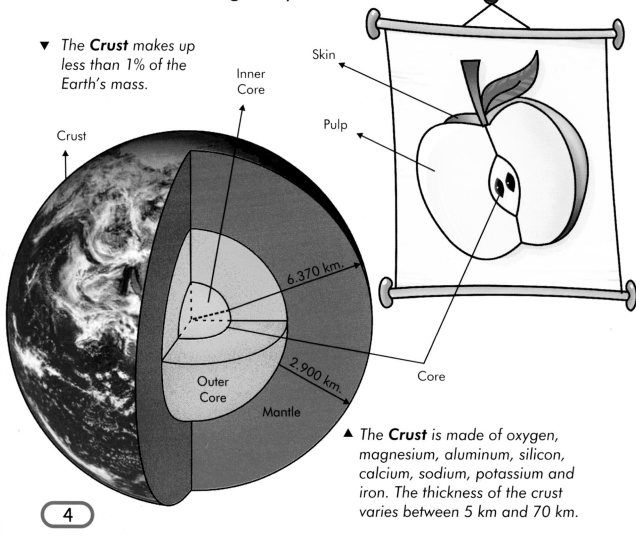

▼ The **Crust** makes up less than 1% of the Earth's mass.

Crust

Inner Core

Skin

Pulp

6.370 km.

2.900 km.

Outer Core

Mantle

Core

▲ The **Crust** is made of oxygen, magnesium, aluminum, silicon, calcium, sodium, potassium and iron. The thickness of the crust varies between 5 km and 70 km.

▼ The **Core** is mainly made of iron and nickel and makes up about 30% of the Earth's mass. The Outer Core is 2200 kms. thick, and is a liquid, while the Inner Core is 1270 kms. thick, and is solid.

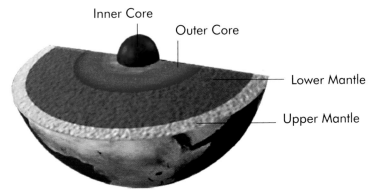

Inner Core

Outer Core

Lower Mantle

Upper Mantle

▲ The **Mantle** is about 3000 kms. thick and makes up about 70% of the Earth's mass. The mantle and crust, is together called, the lithosphere.

▼ There are two types of Crust, **Oceanic Crust** and **Continental Crust**. The first one is about 6-11 kms. thick and mainly consists of heavy rocks, like basalt and dolerite. The Continental Crust is about 19 miles thick, and is mainly made up of light material like granite, and sandstone.

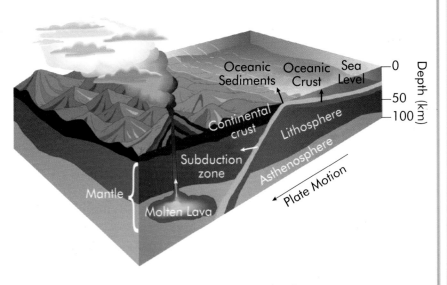

Oceanic Sediments Oceanic Crust Sea Level 0

Continental crust

Lithosphere

Subduction zone

Asthenosphere

Mantle

Molten Lava

Plate Motion

Depth (km) 50 100

Eurasia

North America

South America

Africa

India

Antarctica Australia

Pangaea is a supercontinent that existed from Earth about 300-200 million years ago.

Due to the **Continental Drift**, continents are continuously moving away from each other.

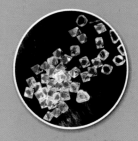

Diamonds are formed by the tremendous heat and pressures within the Earth's crust.

Earth's Atmosphere

The layer of air surrounding the planet Earth is known as the Earth's atmosphere. The atmosphere not only provides us with oxygen to breathe, but also protects us from harmful ultra-violet rays coming from the Sun. The atmosphere has layers which rise and fall with the temperature as the air gets thinner.

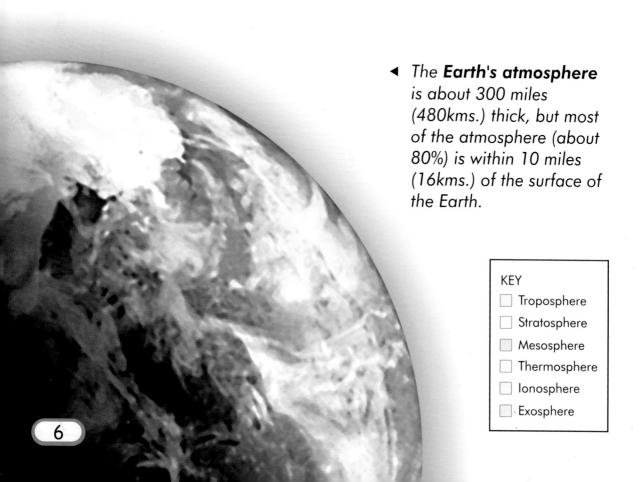

◀ The **Earth's atmosphere** is about 300 miles (480kms.) thick, but most of the atmosphere (about 80%) is within 10 miles (16kms.) of the surface of the Earth.

KEY
- ☐ Troposphere
- ☐ Stratosphere
- ☐ Mesosphere
- ☐ Thermosphere
- ☐ Ionosphere
- ☐ Exosphere

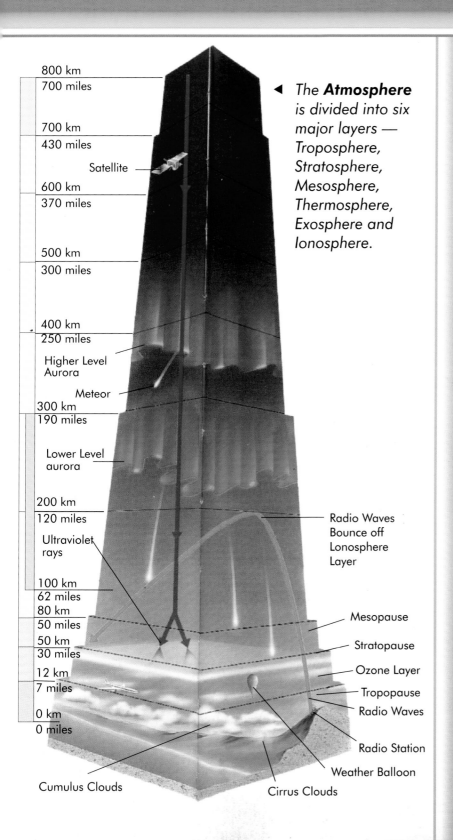

The **Atmosphere** is divided into six major layers — Troposphere, Stratosphere, Mesosphere, Thermosphere, Exosphere and Ionosphere.

800 km
700 miles

700 km
430 miles

Satellite

600 km
370 miles

500 km
300 miles

400 km
250 miles

Higher Level Aurora

Meteor

300 km
190 miles

Lower Level aurora

200 km
120 miles

Ultraviolet rays

100 km
62 miles
80 km
50 miles

50 km
30 miles

12 km
7 miles

0 km
0 miles

Radio Waves Bounce off Lonosphere Layer

Mesopause

Stratopause

Ozone Layer

Tropopause

Radio Waves

Radio Station

Weather Balloon

Cirrus Clouds

Cumulus Clouds

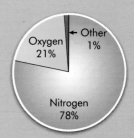

The Earth's atmosphere is composed mainly of **nitrogen and oxygen**.

The **Ozone layer** protects us from the ultraviolet rays of the Sun.

The **Ionosphere** helps in the transmission of radio waves.

Seasons Of The Earth

We experience season because the Earth spins all its axis and at the same time also revolves around the sun. Also the axis has a tilt of 23.5° from the vertical. When the northern part of the Earth is towards the sun, it has summer, when the southern part is away from the sun, it has winter. And after six months, the northern part is away from the sun, it has winter while, the southern part is exposed to the sun, it has summer. This is how season change all through 365 days in a year. But if 0.25 days is add then in the month of February we have a leap year.

▶ If the Earth did not **tilt**, countries near the poles would be cold and dark all the year round.

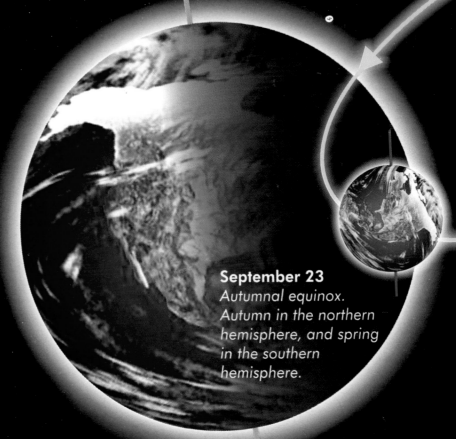

September 23
Autumnal equinox.
Autumn in the northern hemisphere, and spring in the southern hemisphere.

▼ The Earth has four **seasons**. These are Winter, Summer, Autumn and Spring.

March 21
Vernal equinox. Spring in the northern hemisphere, and autumn in the southern hemisphere.

June 21
Summer solstice in the northern hemisphere

Alaska

Alaska has sunshine 24 hours a day during their summertime.

SUN

Earth's Orbit

Equator

Countries near the **Equator** have only two seasons—rainy and dry.

December 22
Winter solstice in the northern hemisphere.

Did you Know?

The planet, **Uranus** is so tilted that its winter lasts for 42 years in which it is in total darkness.

Weather

Weather is the conditions in the atmosphere near the Earth's surface. These conditions include the temperature of the air, air pressure, amount of water in the air known as humidity and the speed of the wind.

*The Sun plays the vital part in causing the weather and its heat is known as **solar**. It absorbs by the Earth, which warm as a result.*

After that the heat passes out from the Earth to the air above, which also turns warmer.

The Sun's rays have the strongest effect around the middle of the Earth (the equator). But, when away from the equator, the sun's rays do not strike directly, therefore the heat is spread over a large area and thus weakening its effect.

The atmosphere presses down on the Earth's surface, creating the **atmospheric pressure**. When warm air rises from the surface, more air moves in from the higher pressure areas, while lower pressure areas from as cooler air pushes down the surface and the air moves.

Wind turbine can be used as a source of electricity.

The circulation of warm and cold current of air is known as **convection** and the current are called as **convection currents**.

Air pressure decreases as we move up in the atmosphere.

Around the Earth there are areas of pressure and these areas are known as **belts**. However, winds don't blow straight from one belt to the other, instead they are deflected sideways from the Earth's rotation, known as **Coriolls effect**.

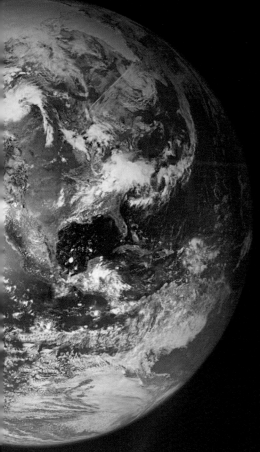

Tiros was the world's first weather satellite launched in 1960.

Climate

Pattern of weather conditions and temperature over a long period of time determine on area's climate. It depends on distance from the sea, latitude and height above sea level.

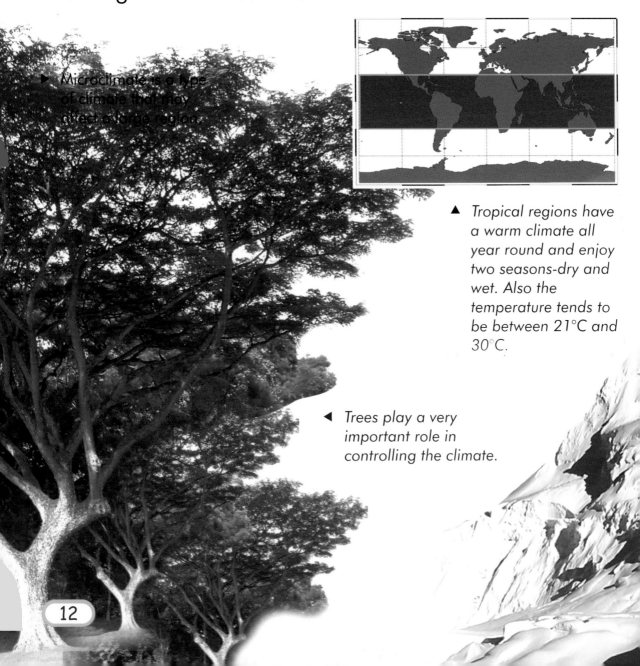

▶ Microclimate is a type of climate that may affect a large region.

▲ Tropical regions have a warm climate all year round and enjoy two seasons-dry and wet. Also the temperature tends to be between 21°C and 30°C.

◀ Trees play a very important role in controlling the climate.

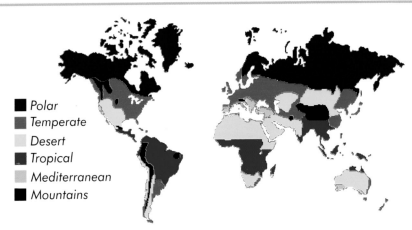

Polar
Temperate
Desert
Tropical
Mediterranean
Mountains

Plants like moss and lichens grow on the high mountain climate.

▲ Climatic region is a large area on the Earth within which the climate is mostly the same. All of the climatic regions have different climate.

◄ Tundra in located on the top of the world near the north pole. This region has harsh wind and low winter temperature from–30°C to –6°C and 25°C.

Citrus fruits grow well in the mediterranean climate.

▼ In mountain areas, temperature drop as height above see level increases, due to which trees can't survive on high mountain slopes for there is little soil.

People of North America have hot summers.

13

Clouds

Clouds are made of small droplets of water and ice. When these drops get too big and heavy to stay in the cloud, they fall on the Earth surface in the form of rainfall. The different types of clouds are formed by the condensation of water above the Earth's surface and can take between few minutes or hours to form a cloud.

Cirrostratus
Thin and wispy clouds in the form of sheets located above an attitude 18,000 feet.

Cumulonimbus
formed near the ground to above 50,000 feet, and can cause lightings, thunder, hail, rains, strong winds, and tornadoes.

Altocumulus
Medium sized scattered clouds formed at 6,500 to 20,000 feet.

Cumulus
often form high in the sky in warm, summer weather.

Cirrus
This is mostly composed of ice crystals and are formed above 18,000 feet.

Cirrocumulus
Clouds with a wave like appearance, located above 18, 000 feet.

Altostratus

Thin and uniform clouds formed at an height of 6,500 to 20,000 feet.

Stratus
Broad and flat clouds, located below 6,500 feet.

Nimbostratus
Uniform, dark flat, low clouds that produce precipitation. Located below 6,500 feet.

Sleet is a kind of frozen raindrops.

Virga is a kind of rain that turns back into water vapour before reaching the ground.

Waterspout is a type of tornado formed at the bottom of a cloud to the surface.

Soil

Soil makes up the outermost layer of the planet Earth. It is a complex mixture of organic matter and minerals. The organic matter, which is also known as *humus* comes from the dead and decaying plants or animals. Soil is formed from the weathering of rocks.

◄ An average **soil sample** is 45 percent minerals, 25 percent water, 25 percent air, and five percent organic matter. Different-sized mineral particles, such as sand, silt, and clay, give the soil its texture.

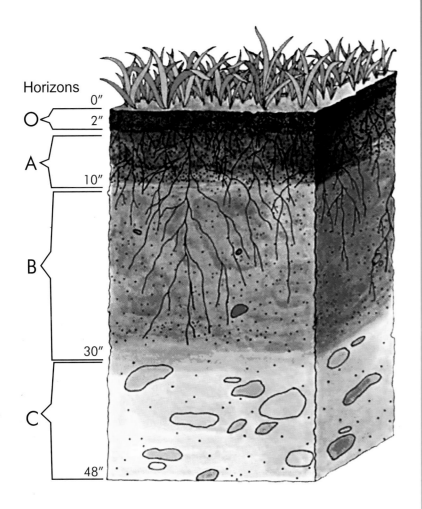

Horizons

O

A

B

C

0"
2"

10"

30"

48"

The Soil is full of **mirco organisms** that eat the decaying matter and release nutrients for plants.

Soil texture refers to the different sizes of mineral particles present in the soil.

▲ If you look in a soil pit or on a roadside cut, you will see various layers in the soil. These layers are called **soil horizons**. Soil horizons differ in a number of easily seen soil properties such as colour, texture, structure, and thickness.

Did you Know?

There are more small living **organisms** in a tablespoon of soil than there are people living on the Earth.

Rocks

Rocks are found all around us. They make up the backbones of hills and mountains, and the foundations of plains and valleys. Rocks are divided into three basic types, Igneous, Sedimentary and Metamorphic, depending upon how they were formed.

▼ **Igneous Rocks** are formed from hot, molten rock that crystallizes and solidifies. Granite, Mica and Quartz are examples of Igneous Rocks.

▶ The Igneous Rocks make up approximately ninety five percent of the upper part of the Earth's crust.

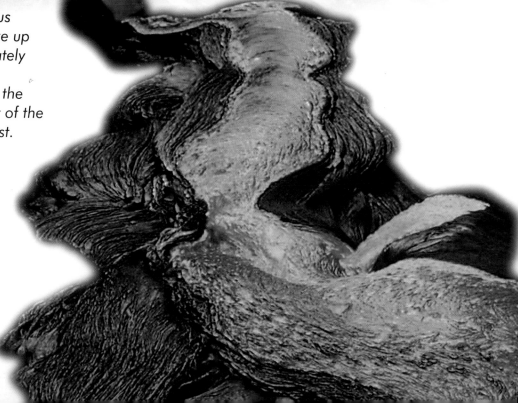

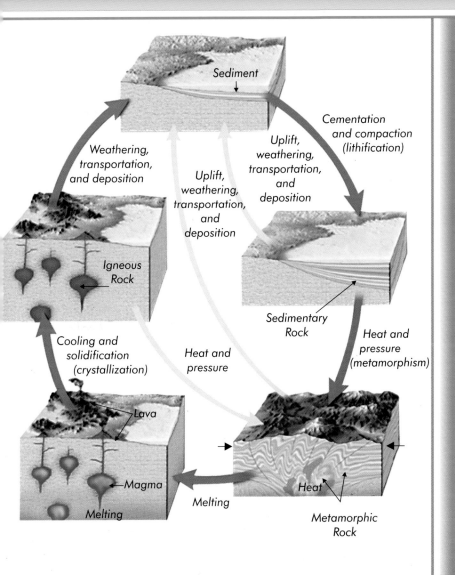

Sediment

Weathering, transportation, and deposition

Uplift, weathering, transportation, and deposition

Uplift, weathering, transportation, and deposition

Cementation and compaction (lithification)

Igneous Rock

Sedimentary Rock

Cooling and solidification (crystallization)

Heat and pressure

Heat and pressure (metamorphism)

Lava

Magma

Melting

Melting

Heat

Metamorphic Rock

Pumice is a special type of rock that floats on water.

Sedimentary Rocks can be easily identified by the presence of layers in it.

▲ The **Rock Cycle** is a group of changes. Igneous Rock can change into Sedimentary Rock or into the Metamorphic Rock. Sedimentary Rock can change into Metamorphic Rock or into Igneous Rock. The Metamorphic Rock can further convert into Igneous or Sedimentary Rock.

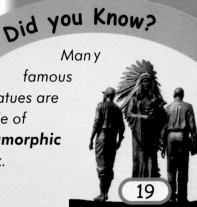

Did you Know?

Many famous statues are made of **Metamorphic Rock**.

19

Rivers And Lakes

Rivers are flowing bodies of water where as a lake, is usually a fresh water body, surrounded by land. There are rivers on every continent except Antarctica, and are an important part of the Earth's water cycle and the sculpting of the Earth's topography as they carry huge quantities of water from the land to the sea. They generally begin at a source, like the snows or a large sheet of ice called the glacier or a natural spring.

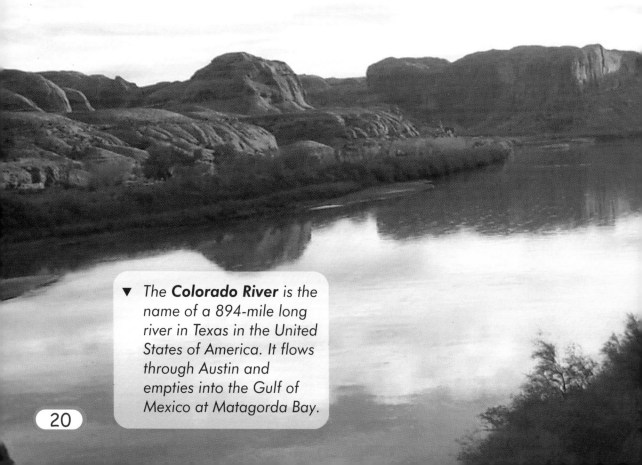

▼ The **Colorado River** is the name of a 894-mile long river in Texas in the United States of America. It flows through Austin and empties into the Gulf of Mexico at Matagorda Bay.

Baikal lake

The oldest and deepest lake on the Earth is Lake Baikal, situated in Russia.

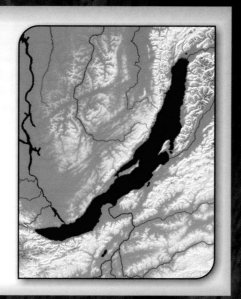

River Nile in North East in Africa is the longest river on planet Earth. Its length's is 6690 km.

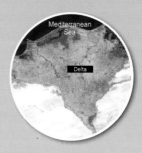

A **delta** is a group of sandy island at the mouth of a river.

Did you Know?

The **Amazon** in South America has the largest drainage area, more than any other river on the planet, Earth.

Oceans

The Oceans of Earth are unique in our Solar System. No other planet in our Solar System has liquid water. Life on Earth first originated in oceans. Oceans covered about two-third of the Earth's surface. The oceans of the Earth serve many functions, particularly affecting the weather and the temperature.

◄ *There are four main types of oceans. They are the* **Pacific Ocean, Atlantic Ocean, Indian Ocean and Arctic Ocean.** *The Pacific is the largest of the four main oceans. There is also the Southern Ocean.*

▼ *The* **oceans** *cover about 71 percent of the Earth's surface, and contain 97 percent of the Earth's water.*

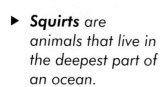

▶ **Squirts** are animals that live in the deepest part of an ocean.

Ninety percent of all **volcanic** activity occurs in the oceans.

▼ the **Blue whale** that lives in oceans is one of the largest animals on planet, Earth.

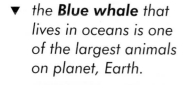

Nearly one-third of the world's **oil** comes from the offshore fields in our oceans.

Did you Know?

The high salt content of the **Dead Sea** allows you to float on the water surface.

Mountains

Mountains are of four types- fold, block, volcanic and residual. All mountains have steep slopes. They are formed by volcanism, erosion, and disturbances or uplifts in the Earth's crust. Mountains occur more often in oceans than on land; some islands are the peaks of mountains coming out of the water.

▲ The *Himalayan Mountain* ranges have been formed by the compression that accompanied collision of the Indian plate with the Eurasian plate.

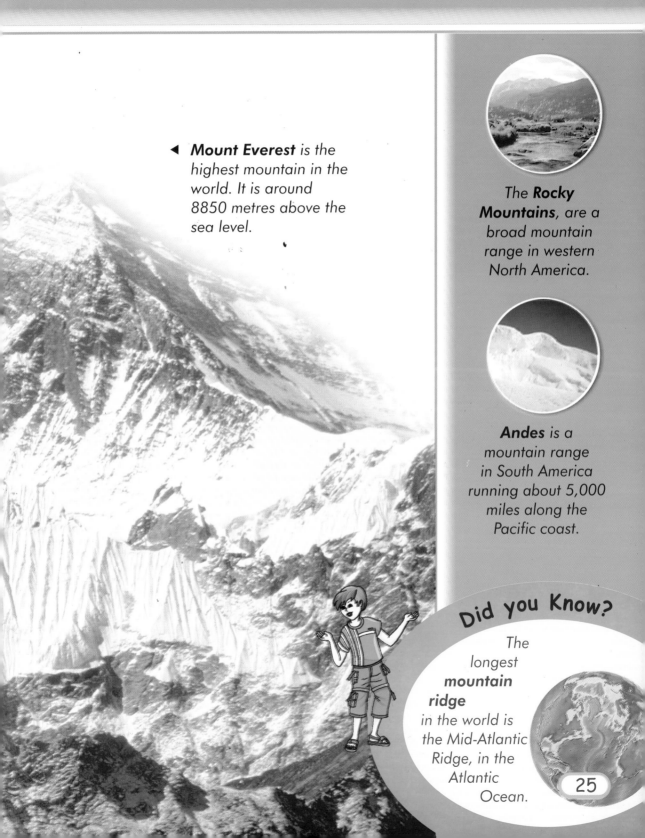

◄ **Mount Everest** is the highest mountain in the world. It is around 8850 metres above the sea level.

The **Rocky Mountains**, are a broad mountain range in western North America.

Andes is a mountain range in South America running about 5,000 miles along the Pacific coast.

Did you Know?

The longest **mountain ridge** in the world is the Mid-Atlantic Ridge, in the Atlantic Ocean.

Islands

An island is a piece of land that is surrounded by water on all sides. Earth is a home to over 100,000 islands. A group of 150 largest islands have been found to be equal to the size of the continent of Europe.

◄ *Mangrove forests are often located on **Tropical Islands**. They act as a buffer to the coastline and are nurseries for the diverse species of fish. Greenland is the largest island in terms of area covering 2,175,600 (km²)*

▼ ***Wake Island** is a volcanic island that has become an atoll. **Atoll** is a kind of island surrounded by coral reefs.*

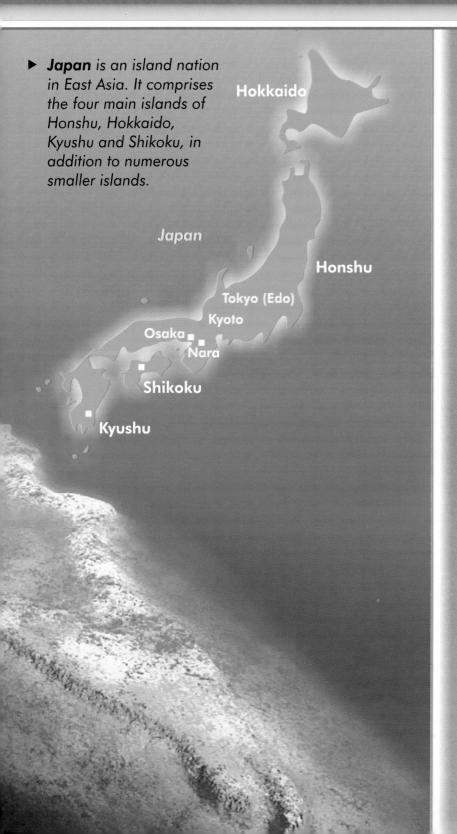

▶ **Japan** is an island nation in East Asia. It comprises the four main islands of Honshu, Hokkaido, Kyushu and Shikoku, in addition to numerous smaller islands.

Hokkaido

Japan

Honshu

Tokyo (Edo)

Kyoto

Osaka

Nara

Shikoku

Kyushu

A chain of islands is called **Archipelago**.

Palm Island in Dubai is one of the largest artificial island in the world.

Barrier Island is an arrow shaped island that forms offshore from a coastline.

27

Glaciers

Glaciers are made up of fallen snow that over many years thickened into large ice masses. What makes glaciers unique is their ability to move. Due to sheer mass, glaciers flow like very slow rivers. Some of the glaciers are as small as football fields, while others grow to be over a hundred kilometres long.

▼ *Glaciers* form when snow remains in one location for a long period of time.

▼ Once a mass of **Glaciers** reaches a critical thickness of around 18 metres, it becomes so heavy that it begins to deform. This causes the glaciers to flow very slowly.

▼ *Glacial ice* often appears blue when it has become very dense, and the ice absorbs all other colours in the spectrum and reflects primarily the blue colour, which is what we see.

Ice Bergs are broken parts of the glaciers.

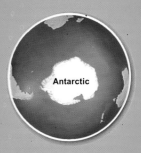

Antarctic

The **Antarctic** ice is over 4,200 metres thick in some areas.

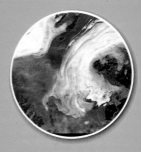

The **Bering Glacier** is the longest and largest glacier in North America.

29

Earthquakes

Earthquakes are caused by the movement in the Earth's crust. Earthquakes happen everyday around the world, but most of them go unnoticed and cause no damage as they are very weak but, large earthquakes can cause serious destruction in the form of building collapse.

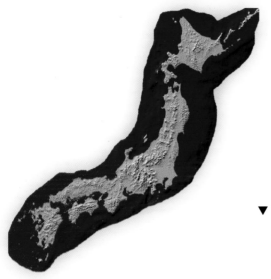

◄ *Japan is one of the world's most seismically active country where more than 20 percent of the earthquake takes place.*

▼ *Focus is the point where energy is suddenly released and an earthquake starts.*

► *Epicenter is the point on the earth's surface that is directly above the point where an earthquake occurs. Vibrations called seismic waves travel from the focus in all directions.*

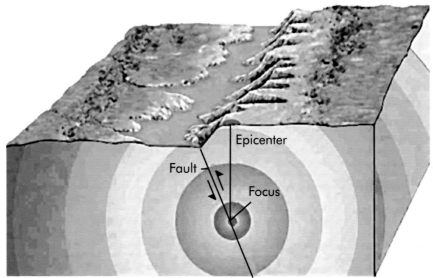

Epicenter

Fault

Focus

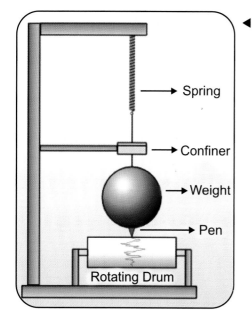

Spring

Confiner

Weight

Pen

Rotating Drum

◀ **Seismometer** *is an instrument that senses the earth motion. Calculations are made from several seismograph, both close to and far from the center of earthquake. It is said that animals behaviours may also be used or seen as to predict an earthquake.*

Earthquake *is recorded on seismograph.*

Tsunamis *are large ocean waves that occurs inside the sea due to earthquake.*

▼ *The earth's surface is made up of a series of large plates called* **tectonic plates**. *These plates are in constant motion travelling at a few centimetres per year. The edges of these plates, where they move against each other, are sites of intense geologic activity, such as earthquakes, volcanoes, and mountain building.*

Charles Richter *developed Richter Scale to measure the intensity of earthquake.*

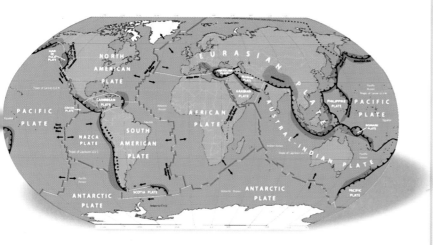

Volcanoes

A Volcano is a vent in the Earth's crust through which melted lava and gases are ejected. Eruptions can cause lateral blasts, lava flows, hot ash flows, mudslides, avalanches, falling ash and floods. Volcano eruptions have been known to knock down many forests. An erupting volcano can trigger *tsunamis, flashfloods, earthquakes, mudflows* and *rock falls*. Most Volcanoes form along plate boundaries or under the sea.

◄ *Volcanic Ash are made up of pulverized rocks that can be harsh, acidic and smelly.*

▶ *The explosive effect of **lava** is known as eruption.*

▼ The **Island of Hawaii** is composed of five volcanoes, two of which Mauna Loa and Kilauea have erupted repeatedly in this century. Another of the volcanoe, Hualalai, erupted in 1801 and has the potential to erupt again within our lifetime.

When Magma comes out of earth's surface it is Known as **Lava**.

Kaua'i

O' ahu

Molokai

Lana'i

Maui

Hawaii' Island

Most of the volcanoes are located around the edge of the Pacific Ocean, in a band called the "**Ring of Fire.**"

Hawaii

▼ **Aniakchak Caldera** formed during an enormous volcanic explosive eruption that expelled more than 50 km^3 of magma about 3,450 years ago. The caldera is 10 km in diameter and 500-1,000 m deep.

Lava fountain is a common feature on Hawaiian volcanoes.

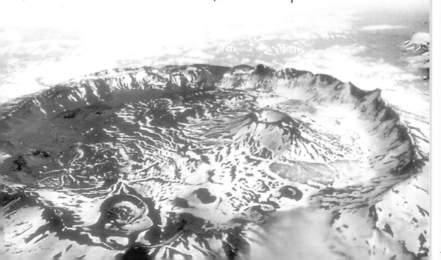

Storms

A storm is a kind of disturbance on the Earth's atmosphere. It strongly affects the weather conditions and are created when a centre of low pressure develops, with a system of high pressure surrounding it. This combination of opposing forces can create strong winds, and result in the formation of storm clouds, such as the *cumulonimbus*.

▼ *Hurricanes* are a type of cyclones with heavy rainfall and winds moving with a speed of more than 80 km. per hour.

◀ A **Cyclone** is a low pressure zone around which the wind blows in counter clock wise direction.

Dust devils are swirls that go upward to fizzle out in clear air.

▼ A **Tornado** is a type of storm resulting from strong rising of air currents. It is associated with heavy rainfall along with thunder and lightning.

Waterspout is a column of rotating wind that reach heights of up to 10,000 feet.

◀ It is also believed by the scientist that **swirling clouds** over the sea indicates impending storms.

A **Blizzard** is a violent snowstorm, where winds blow at a speed of about 100 kms. per hour.

Fossils

Fossils are the remains of plants and animals embedded in rocks. Fossils are typically preserved when they are buried under many layers of sand and mud. Fossils have the same shape that the original item had, but their colour, density, and texture vary widely.

▶ *Three small **Ammonite Fossils** each measuring 1.5 c.m in size.*

◀ *The first **Archaeopteryx Fossil**, which was a feather, was found in 1860 near Solnhofen, Germany, and was named by the German paleontologist, Hermann Von Meyer in 1861. That year he also discovered the first specimen of Archaeopteryx.*

A fossil of **trilobite**.

▲ **Fossils** are generally found in Sedimentary Rocks formed by soft silts and muds. The soft sediment preserves the fine details in the bones, teeth, and other body parts.

Orthoceras is a 400 million old fossil of a cephalopod.

Fossils are mainly found in **Sedimentary Rocks**.

▲ A **fossil of fish** obtained from Utah, North America.

Forests

A forest is an area with a large number of trees. It provides shelter to different kinds of animals. A wide variety of food, medicine and wood is obtained from the forests. It cover about 30 percent of the Earth's total surface area.

▼ *Rainforests* are a home to more than 50% of all the living organisms. Once rainforests covered 14% of the Earth's surface, now it covers only 6% of the total Earth's surface.

▶ **Rings** are the characteristic features of a trees. The age of a tree can be calculated by counting the number of rings present in the tree.

▼ **Bristlecone Pine** is the oldest living tree in the world. Some of the trees are 5,000 year old.

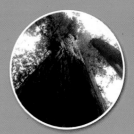

Redwood is the longest tree on Earth with a height up to 400 feet.

Bamboo which seems to be a tree is actually a type of grass.

The **Amazon Forests** provide 20% of the world's fresh oxygen.

39

First Life On Earth

Earth was lifeless when it was formed some 4.6 billion years ago. One billion year later, it was packed with prokaryotic life forms, ancestors of all present living things. Prokaryotes are group of very small animals whose body is composed of simple types of cells without any nucleus.

▶ *The **early Earth** was heavily bombarded by the Solar System materials, such as comets and asteroid-sized objects.*

▶ The first single celled organism appeared on Earth 3500 million years ago in the Precambrian Era.

▶ Reptiles evolved during the Permian Period as they were able to spread all over the world because land joined as a huge continent and insects and millipedes were also able to move onto the land. This was possible for the Earth's temperature had cooled enough for land plants to row in large number providing food.

▶ Hylonomus was one of the earliest known reptiles.

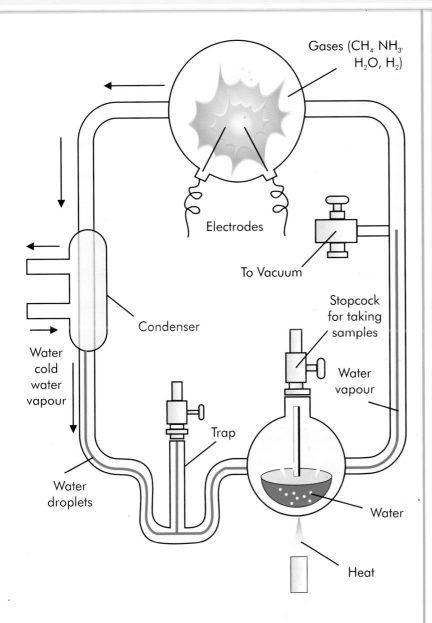

Gases (CH$_4$, NH$_3$, H$_2$O, H$_2$)

Electrodes

To Vacuum

Condenser

Stopcock for taking samples

Water cold water vapour

Water vapour

Water droplets

Trap

Water

Heat

Earth's early atmosphere was mainly composed of **nitrogen and methane.**

The **microbes** were responsible for the production of most of the Earth's oxygen.

Stromatolites are the oldest known fossils, dating back to more than 3 billion years.

▲ The **Miller-Urey experiment** attempts to recreate the chemical conditions of the primitive Earth in the laboratory, and synthesized some of the building blocks of life. This experiment is considered to be the classic experiment on the origin of life. It was conducted in 1953 by Stanley L. Miller and Harold C. Urey at the University of Chicago.

Extinct Animals of the Earth

The dinosaurs were among the most successful animals that ever lived on Earth. The first dinosaurs appeared on Earth about 230 million years ago. They lived in nearly all natural settings, from open plains to forests, to the edges of swamps, lakes, and oceans. Then about 65 million years ago, the dinosaurs died out.

▶ Growing to a height of 15 feet, **mammoths** were the largest of the group of animals called Proboscidea, which also includes mastodons and elephants. They lived from about 2 million years ago to 9,000 years ago.

▼ **Dunkleosteus** was primitive fish that lived about 360 million years ago. Its fossils have been found in Morocco, Africa, Poland, Belgium, China, and the USA.

▶ Ichthyosaurus was a giant reptile that lived on Earth roughly 206 to 140 million years ago.

▼ **Brontosaurus** was one of the largest land animals that ever existed. This enormous plant-eater measured about 70-90 feet long, and about 15 feet tall at the hips. It weighed roughly 33-38 tons.

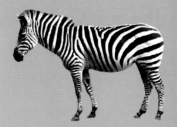

The **Quagga** is a recently-extinct relative of the zebra.

The **dodo** is an extinct, flightless bird that lived on an island in the Indian Ocean near Africa.

Glyptodon was a car-sized amadillo.

Earth's Resources

All over the world, people use resources which are buried beneath the Earth's surface. Many of the stones and metals are used today for various constructions in building, offices etc.

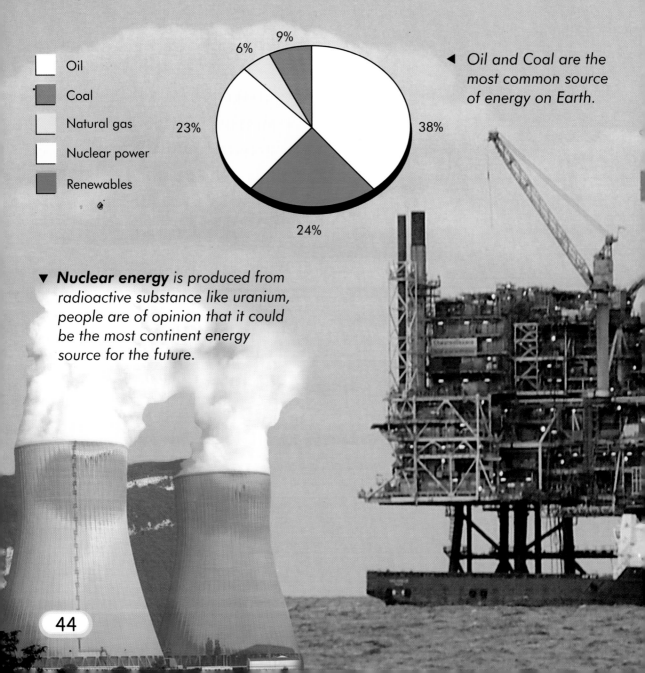

Oil

Coal

Natural gas

Nuclear power

Renewables

9%

6%

23%

38%

24%

◀ *Oil and Coal are the most common source of energy on Earth.*

▼ **Nuclear energy** *is produced from radioactive substance like uranium, people are of opinion that it could be the most continent energy source for the future.*

▶ **Ores** are minerals or rocks from which different metals are obtained. Ores often comes in different colours due to the presence of different metals in it.

◀ **Petroleum refineries** in the oceans are one of the main source of fossil fuels.

Solar power provide clean form of energy

Drink cans can be melted and re-used again like coke cans.

Precious stones are used in jewellery.

Deserts

Deserts are places on earth that are characterized by little vegetation and rain. It receives less than 10 inches of rainfall annually. It loses more water through evaporation than it gains from precipitation. They are typically characterized by extremely hot daytime temperatures, and have plant that are adapted to low moisture conditions. Deserts cover about one-fifth of the entire land area in the world.

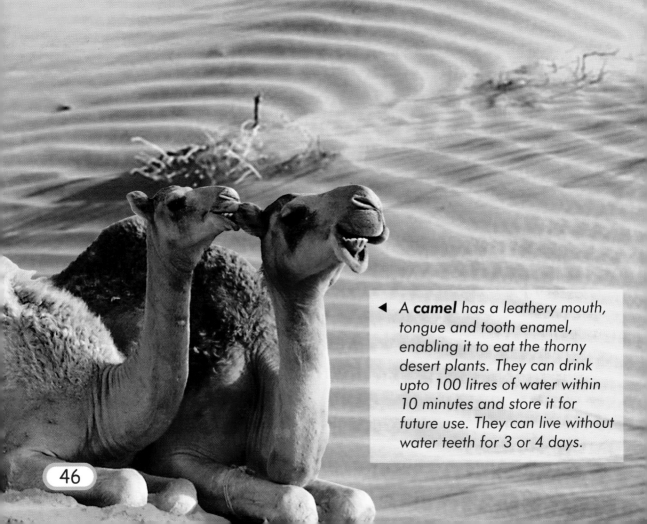

◄ A **camel** has a leathery mouth, tongue and tooth enamel, enabling it to eat the thorny desert plants. They can drink upto 100 litres of water within 10 minutes and store it for future use. They can live without water teeth for 3 or 4 days.

▶ The **Kangaroo Rat** is a very cute little creature that looks like a mini kangaroo, but is as big as a mouse. It can live upto 3 - 5 years without taking a single sip of water.

Oases are parts of the desert where plants grow, and water is almost always available here.

Atacama Desert
The driest place in the world is the Atacama Desert in Chile for it receives an annual rainfall of only 0.51 mm.

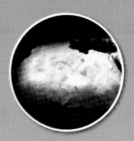

A satellite image of the **Sahara**, the world's largest hot desert.

▶ **Grasses** can be found here and there and serve as the main source of water for animals living in deserts.

The Saguaro one of the largest **cactus** found in deserts.

Glossary

Ammonite: One of the coiled chambered fossil shells of extinct mollusks.

Archaeopteryx: A prehistoric reptile with limbs which resembled the wings of today's birds. It is considered a primary link in the evolutionary process between the ancient reptiles of millions of years ago, and birds as we know them now.

Artificial Island: An island that has been formed by humans, rather than by natural means.

Cactus: A plant with succulent stems and leaves.

Cephalopod: Marine invertebrates characterized by a head surrounded by tentacles and, in most fossil forms, by the presence of a straight or spirally coiled, calcareous shell divided into numerous interior chambers.

Continental Drift: Widely accepted view that the continents of the Earth are slowly drifting across the surface of the globe.

Deform: To alter the shape of something.

Drainage area: The place where the run-off water goes when passing beneath a bridge or passing a specific location in a river or stream.

Eclipse: Effect caused by one body casting a shadow on another.

Epicenter: Point on the surface of the Earth located above the earthquake hypocenter (or focus).

Erosion: The wearing away of land or soil by the action of wind, water or ice.

Ionosphere: The part of the Earth's atmosphere beginning at an altitude of about 50 kilometres (30 miles) and extending outwards to about 500 kilometres (300 miles) or more.

Humus: A general term for the more or less decomposed plant and animal residues in the lower organic soil layer.

Igneous Rocks: Rocks formed by the solidification of molten material from far below the Earth's surface.

Magnetic field: All magnetic fields are created by the moving electric charge.

Mesosphere: Region of the atmosphere between 50 and 85 kms approximately.

Metamorphic Rocks: Rocks whose physical and chemical properties have been changed by the elevated temperature and pressure.

Mountain range: A series of hills or mountains.

Natural satellite: A body of lesser mass, formed without human intervention, revolving about a planet (or object) of greater mass.

Ozone layer: The protective layer in the atmosphere, about 1 5 miles above the ground, that absorbs some of the sun's ultraviolet rays, thereby reducing the amount of potentially harmful radiation that reaches the Earth's surface.

Revolution: The motion of one body around another.

DISCOVER THE WORLD

THE PLANTS

Plants are Everywhere

Plants grow everywhere. They grow on land, in the ocean, in lakes and rivers, on mountain tops, and in the desert. Plants are even found in cold climate of Antarctica.

▸ *The largest flower in the world, the Rafflesia arnoldii, weighs 7 kg (15 pounds) and grows only on the Sumatran island of Indonesia.*

◂ **Water Hyacinth** *is one of the fastest water growing plants.*

◂ **Succulent Desert Plants,** *such as the cacti, are able to store water in their thick stems.*

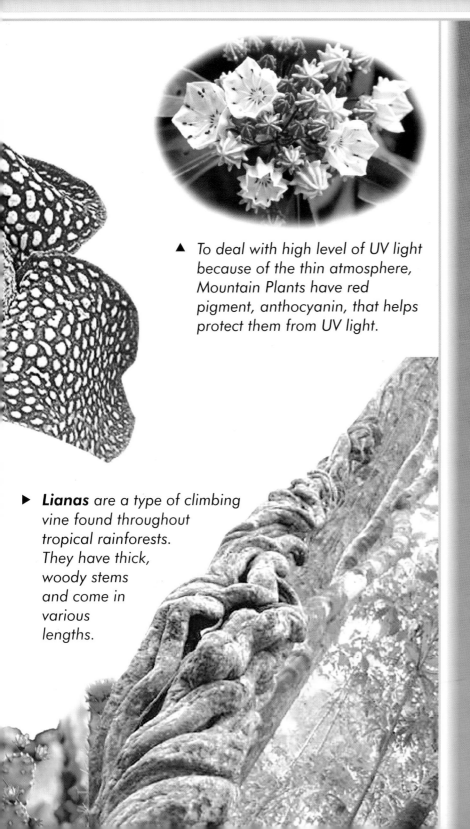

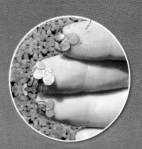

Duckweed is the smallest flower in the world.

▲ To deal with high level of UV light because of the thin atmosphere, Mountain Plants have red pigment, anthocyanin, that helps protect them from UV light.

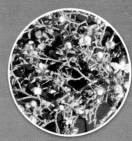

The **Creosote Bush** is found in the Mojave Desert.

▶ **Lianas** are a type of climbing vine found throughout tropical rainforests. They have thick, woody stems and come in various lengths.

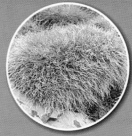

One of the Antarctic plants, Deschampsia antarctica, has adapted to its harsh environment by producing antifreeze proteins.

Importance of Plants

Plants are important because they are the ultimate source of food. Besides food, plants also provide us with wood, fibre, drugs, oils, latex and resins. Thus plants provide people not only sustenance but shelter, clothing, medicines, and the raw materials from which innumerable other products are made.

▶ **Cotton** and other plants provide us with the materials we used to make many of the clothes we wear.

◀ **Coconut** oil is found in soaps, shampoos, and suntan lotions, and is used to make glycerine, which is found in a variety of products including cosmetics and soaps.

▶ Linen, made from the **flax plant**, is used for fine tablecloths, handkerchiefs and napkins.

4

▲ Toothpastes usually contain plant flavourings such as **peppermint**, spearmint, cinnamon, **wintergreen**, or menthol.

▼ Aspirin, which is consumed at a rate of 80 million pills a day in the U.S., was first discovered from a chemical found in **willow trees**.

Quinine, obtained from the bark of the cinchona tree, was one of the most valuable

Cork, from the bark of cork oak, is used for flooring, wine bottle stoppers, insulation, buoys, fishing floats, hotmats, bulletin boards, and cork black used by artists in

Did you Know?

The **wood** from trees is used in the construction of homes.

Types of Plants

There are about 350,000 species of plants.
These include trees, herbs, shrubs, bushes, grasses, vines, ferns, and mosses.

▶ The **Banana tree** is not actually a true tree; it is an herb.

▲ **Ferns** are older than land animals and far older than dinosaurs. They were thriving on Earth two hundred million years before flowering plants evolved.

◀ A Hanukkah bush is not to be mistaken with an actual **Christmas tree.**

▶ The General **Sherman Tree** in Sequoia National Park is the largest (by volume) tree in the world.

▼ **Annual rings** of a tree can tell the age of a tree.

Bamboo is not a tree, it is a giant grass.

Mosses are small, soft plants that are typically 1–10 cm tall.

Shrubs are **woody plants** smaller than trees, having a short stem with branches near the ground.

Parts of Plants

Most plants have two basic parts. Let us find out what they are and what they do for the plant.

- ▶ The root which grows under the ground anchors the plant to the soil and helps the plant to absorb water and nutrients from the soil.

- ▶ The shoot which grows above the ground, holds up the branches. Leaves, flowers and fruits grow on branches.

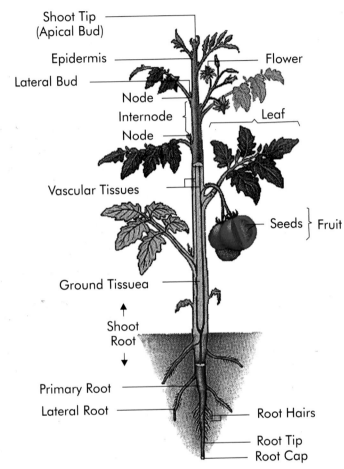

Shoot Tip (Apical Bud)
Epidermis
Lateral Bud
Node
Internode
Node
Vascular Tissues
Ground Tissuea
Shoot
Root
Primary Root
Lateral Root
Flower
Leaf
Seeds } Fruit
Root Hairs
Root Tip
Root Cap

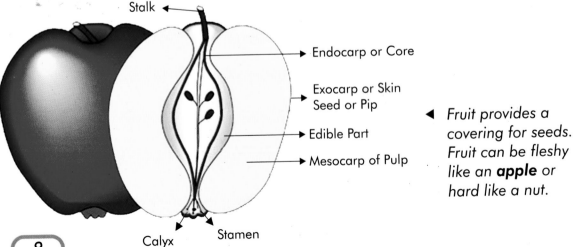

Stalk
Endocarp or Core
Exocarp or Skin
Seed or Pip
Edible Part
Mesocarp of Pulp
Calyx
Stamen

◀ Fruit provides a covering for seeds. Fruit can be fleshy like an **apple** or hard like a nut.

8

▶ Flowers make **fruits**. Fruits hold the seeds of the plant. Some fruits that we eat are: tomatoes, oranges, pears, watermelon, and strawberries.

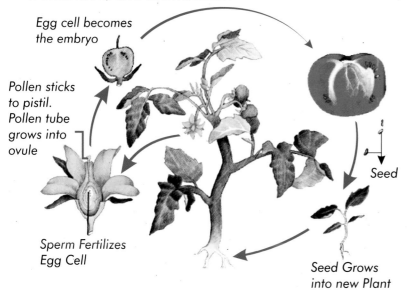

Egg cell becomes the embryo

Pollen sticks to pistil. Pollen tube grows into ovule

Sperm Fertilizes Egg Cell

Seed

Seed Grows into new Plant

Fibrous Roots are very slender with very thin root hair. Grass plants have a fibrous root system.

Taproot is a root with a few branches that is very thick and swollen. Carrots are an example.

▶ These are the reproductive parts of a plant. **Flower** attract insects and bees to pollinate them. After pollination, the petals fall off and seeds develop in the part of a flower called the ovary. The ovary itself usually becomes what we call the fruit.

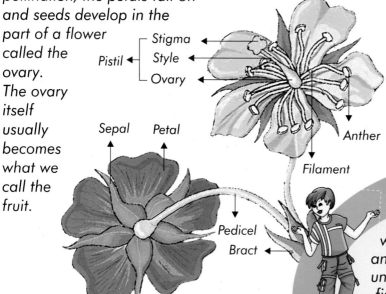

Pistil — Stigma / Style / Ovary

Sepal   Petal

Anther

Filament

Pedicel

Bract

Did you Know?

Seeds contain food which supplies energy and materials for growth until the seeds grow there first leaves.

Flowers

Flower is the reproductive part of the plant. Flower attracts insects and bees to pollinate it. After pollination, the petals fall off and seeds develop in the part of a flower called the ovary. The ovary itself usually becomes what we call the fruit.

▶ *If a flower has a stamen, pistils, petals, and sepals, it is called a complete flower. If one of these parts is missing, the flower is designated incomplete flower.*

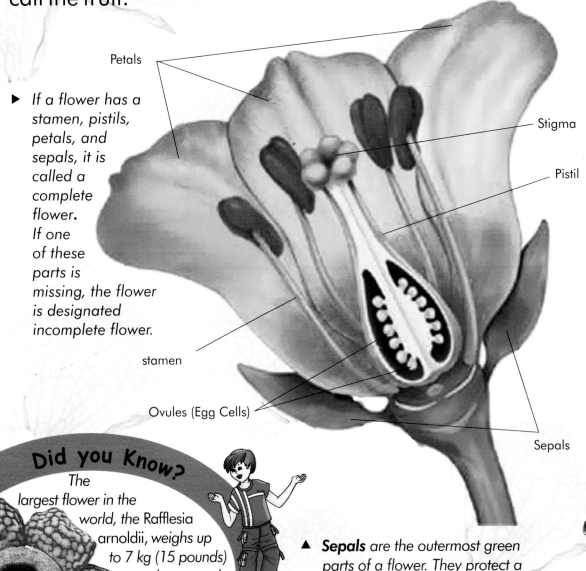

Petals

Stigma

Pistil

stamen

Ovules (Egg Cells)

Sepals

▲ **Sepals** are the outermost green parts of a flower. They protect a flower when it is a bud.

▶ There are different edible flowers which are used as food plants. **Lilac** is used on cakes or confectionary and tea blends.

Petals are highly coloured portions of the flower. They may contain perfume as well as nectar glands. The petals collectively are called the corolla.

The **pistil** is the female part of the plant. It consists of the stigma, style, and ovary.

The **stamen** is the male reproductive organ. It consists of a pollen sac (anther) and a long supporting filament.

◀ Flowers have been symbols of beauty in most civilizations of the world, and gifting flowers is still the most popular tradition at social functions.

Seeds

Plants grow from seeds. Inside each seed is an embryo, or baby plant. The embryo is surrounded by a food storage area. Seeds have a protective outer layer called the seed coat.

▸ **Lotus seeds** up to 2000 years old have survived and germinated.

◀ **Cycas revoluta** from Hawaii has female cones bearing large, orange seeds.

▲ A seed contains an **embryonic plant** in a resting condition, and germination is its resumption of growth. Seeds will begin to germinate when the soil temperature is in the appropriate range and when water and oxygen are available.

Dandelion seeds can be carried long distances by the wind.

▼ **Strawberry fruit** has seeds on its skin rather than inside it.

Juniper berries are not berries but seeds.

Did you Know?

The largest seed in the world is the coco-de-mer.

13

Pollination

Pollination is an important step in the plant reproduction. When pollination occurs, pollen moves from the male parts to the female parts of the plant. As a result of pollination, plants produce seeds. Pollen are dispersed by wind, water and other pollinators such as animals, insects, bees, bats and birds.

▼ ***Insect-pollinated flowers*** *have several ways of attracting insects. These include large colourful petals, scent and nectar.*

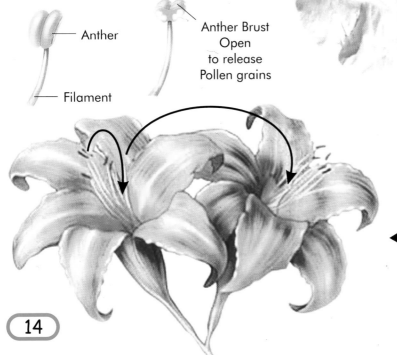

Anther

Anther Brust Open to release Pollen grains

Filament

◄ *If the flowers on two different individual plants are pollinated the flower is said to have been cross-pollinated.*

▶ Almonds, apples, avocados, blueberries, cantaloupes, cherries, cranberries, cucumbers, sunflowers, watermelon and many other crops all rely on honeybees for pollination.

▶ If flowers on the same plant get pollinated, or if the pollen from the stangens of a flower reached the stigma of the same flower. The flower is said to have been self pollinated.

Cycads use scent to lure thrips for pollination.

Pollen is made by the male organs of a plant called anthers.

Wind-pollinated flowers have small petals, no scent, no nectar.

Quiz time!

1. Pollination by wind is called ....

2. Pollination by insect is called ....

3. Pollination by water is called ....

Answers: 1. Anemophily 2. Entomophily 3. Hydrophily

Leaves

A leaf is the food manufacturing organ of plants. A leaf is usually flat and thin which allow sunlight to cover broader area and penetrate deeper into the tissue. Most leaves are green in colour due the presence of chlorophyll.

▶ **Pigments** besides chlorophyll that give a leaf its characteristic color are the carotenoids (orange-red and yellow), the anthocyanins (red, purple, and blue), and the tannins (brown).

◀ The leaves of most **conifers** remain on the tree for 2 to 10 years.

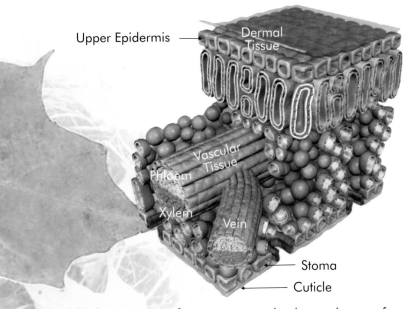

Upper Epidermis — Dermal Tissue

Vascular Tissue

Phloem

Xylem

Vein

— Stoma

— Cuticle

Leaf blade is veined with sap-conducting tubes (xylem and phloem) with thick-walled

▲ The blade consists of an upper and a lower layer of closely-fitted **epidermal cells**, including specialized paired guard cells that control the size of tiny pores, or stomata, for gaseous exchange and the release of water vapor.

▶ **Cotyledons** are the first leaves that are produced from the seed.

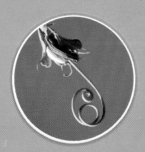

A **tendril** is a specialized leaf with a threadlike shape that is used by climbing plants for support and attachment.

◀ **Desert plants** have very succulent leaves that reduce the loss of water during transpiration.

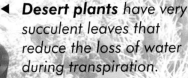

Did you Know?

A **bulb** is an underground vertical shoot that has modified leaves and is used as food storage organs.

17

Fruits and Vegetables

Fruits are that parts of plants which develops from flowers. Nuts, olives, tomatoes, peas and runner beans are all examples of fruits, as well as the obvious ones like apples, oranges and grapes. Vegetables are non-seed containing plant, such as cabbage, onions, and tubers such as potatoes.

▼ **Carambola** also known as starfruit is an excellent source of vitamin C.

▲ **Apricots** contain nutrients such as vitamin A that promote good vision.

▼ **Eggplant** is a fruit we consume as a vegetable.

▶ **Tomatoes** *are very high in the carotenoid; eating foods with carotenoids can lower your risk of cancer.*

*Most of the nutrients in a **potato** reside just below the skin layer.*

◀ **Bananas** *contain three natural sugars — sucrose, fructose and glucose — combined with fiber. A banana gives an instant, sustained and substantial boost of energy.*

Pea *is a vegetable that develops from seeds.*

Quiz time!

1. The king of vegetable is..............

2. Which vitamin is found in citrus fruit?

3. Which fruit is shown in the picture?

Radish *is a vegetable that develops*

Answers: 1. Potato **2.** vitamin C **3.** Apricot

How Plants make Food

Food is essential for all organisms.
Plants need several things to make their own food such as chlorophyll, light, carbon dioxide, water, nutrients and minerals.

▼ **Photosynthesis** is the process by which plants make food.

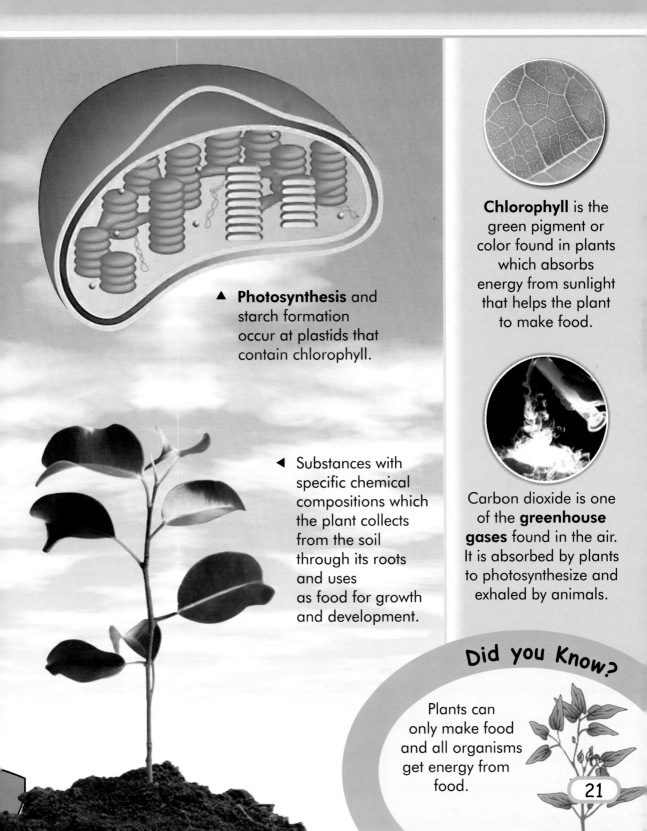

▲ **Photosynthesis** and starch formation occur at plastids that contain chlorophyll.

Chlorophyll is the green pigment or color found in plants which absorbs energy from sunlight that helps the plant to make food.

◀ Substances with specific chemical compositions which the plant collects from the soil through its roots and uses as food for growth and development.

Carbon dioxide is one of the **greenhouse gases** found in the air. It is absorbed by plants to photosynthesize and exhaled by animals.

Did you Know?

Plants can only make food and all organisms get energy from food.

21

Growth of Plants

Plants are living things and like other living things, they also grow and reproduce. For plants to grow healthy they requires some basic factors. Let us discuss what they are.

▼ Water is an important factor for the plant growth. Without water or with too much water, a plant dies. Most plants like to be watered when the soil is slightly dry to the touch.

▼ All plants need space to grow so branches can stretch out and the leaves receive maximum sunlight to carry out the process of making food. Roots also need room to grow. Plants growing in small spaces will have their roots crowded, and that results in stunted of growth.

▼ Seed begins to germinate when the soil temperature is in the appropriate range and when oxygen and water are available.

Plumule is the part of the seed embryo that develops into the shoot.

Radicle is the part of the seed embryo that develops into the root.

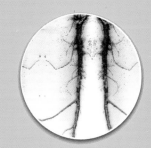

Taproot is a straight tapering root which stores food and water. It forms a center from which root hairs sprout.

Primitive Plants

Early plants were small. Plant body composed of single cell and soft body tissues, with simple branching. These plants also lacked vascular tissue and reproduced by means of spores rather than seeds.

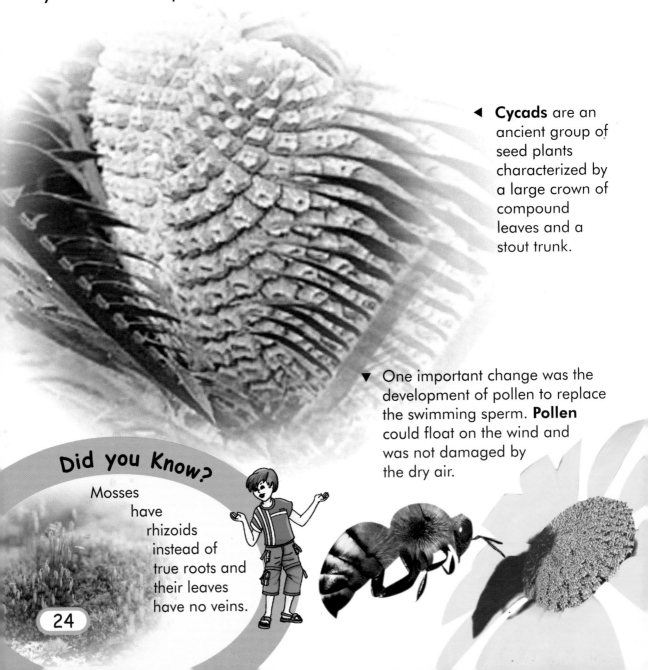

◄ **Cycads** are an ancient group of seed plants characterized by a large crown of compound leaves and a stout trunk.

▼ One important change was the development of pollen to replace the swimming sperm. **Pollen** could float on the wind and was not damaged by the dry air.

Did you Know?

Mosses have rhizoids instead of true roots and their leaves have no veins.

▶ **Ferns** *are a very ancient family of plants: early fern fossils evolved during the Mesozoic era, 360 million years ago.*

The word **"conifer"** means "cone bearing". conifers fear cones which contain their seeds. Conifers spread widely during the Permian age.

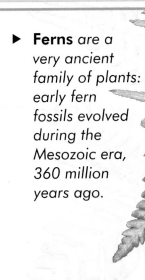

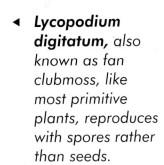

◀ ***Lycopodium digitatum,*** *also known as fan clubmoss, like most primitive plants, reproduces with spores rather than seeds.*

Lycopodium squarrosum, a descendant of the early lycopods.

▼ *The oldest fossils of land plants visible with the naked eye are about 425 million years old. They are miniscule plants from the Mid-Silurian of Ireland en are called* **Cooksonia.**

Mosses are small, soft plants that are typically 110 cm tall, though some species are much larger.

Plant Cell

Plant cells are almost rectangular in shape. Plant cells are like animal cells, but they have a cell wall and chloroplasts. Plant cells are extremely effective at removing excess carbon dioxide from the atmosphere.

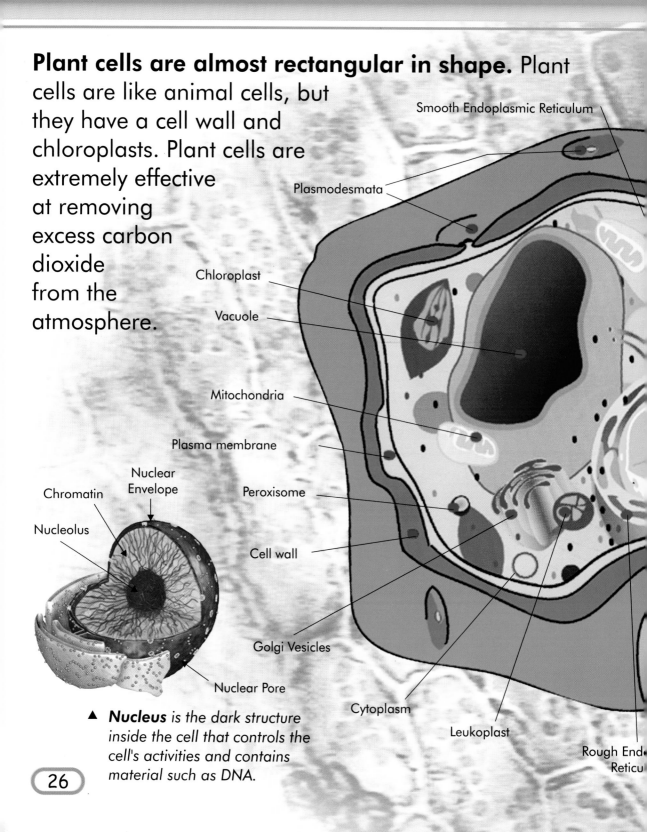

Smooth Endoplasmic Reticulum

Plasmodesmata

Chloroplast

Vacuole

Mitochondria

Plasma membrane

Peroxisome

Cell wall

Chromatin

Nuclear Envelope

Nucleolus

Golgi Vesicles

Nuclear Pore

Cytoplasm

Leukoplast

Rough End
Reticu

▲ **Nucleus** is the dark structure inside the cell that controls the cell's activities and contains material such as DNA.

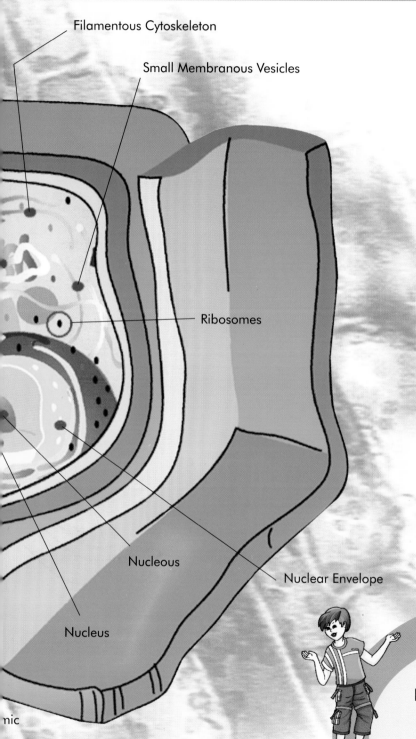

Filamentous Cytoskeleton

Small Membranous Vesicles

Ribosomes

Nucleous

Nuclear Envelope

Nucleus

nic

Ribosomes *participate in protein synthesis.*

Mitochondria *are often referred to as the power plants of the cell because many of the reactions that produce energy take place in the mitochondria.*

Did you Know?

Plants cells are rigid because they have walls of tough cellulose.

27

Vascular Tissue

Vascular tissue consists of xylem and phloem. These two types of vessels run side-by-side, extending from roots to leaves. Xylem conducts water and dissolved minerals and phloem conducts food and other organic substances.

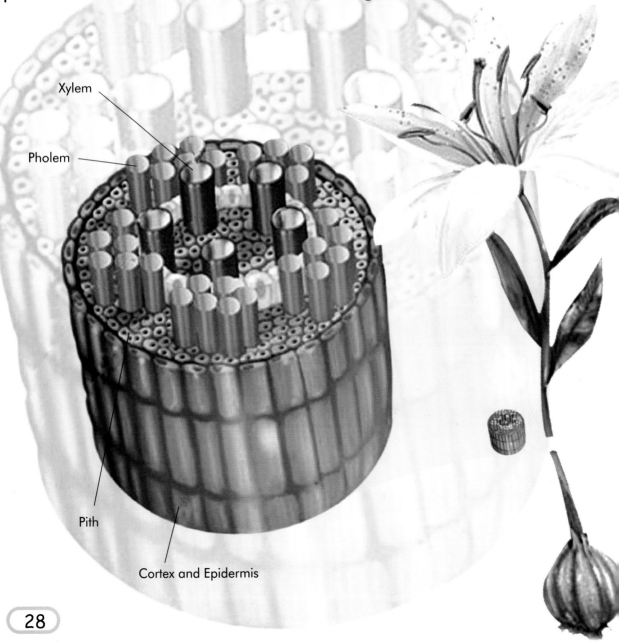

Xylem

Pholem

Pith

Cortex and Epidermis

Sclerenchyma Cells (fibers)

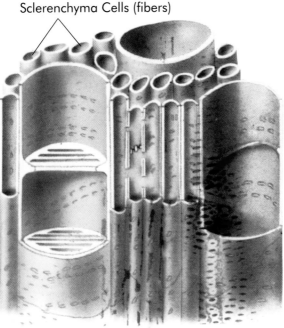

▶ Xylem is one of the transport tissues, phloem being the other. It is found throughout the plant.

The **vein system** of a leaf consists of branched vascular bundles. A vein contains the vascular tissue which consists of xylem and phloem. The lignified xylem cells are situated towards the upper epidermis and the phloem towards the lower epidermis.

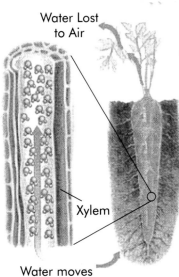

Water Lost to Air

Xylem

Water moves up xylem

◀ The open ends of xylem vessel cells form complete pipelike tubes.

Source of Sugars

Phloem

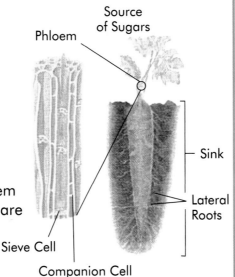

Sink

Lateral Roots

▶ Sugars in the pholem of this carrot plant are moving to sinks.

Sieve Cell

Companion Cell

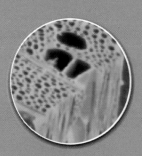

Tracheids are elongated cells in the xylem of vascular plants, serving in the transport of water and minerals.

Aquatic Plants

Aquatic plants are adapted to living in water bodies such as lake, river, pond and ocean. Some simply float on water, while others are partially or totally submerged.

▶ **Lotus** with stunning leaves and flowers standing high above the water, is one the most dramatic pond ornaments of all.

▼ **Victoria amazonica** has floating leaves up to 2 m across.

▶ **Lemna** is a tiny aquatic plant, resembling a floating leaf, 2-3 mm long. Its inflorescence is minute, one of the smallest known.

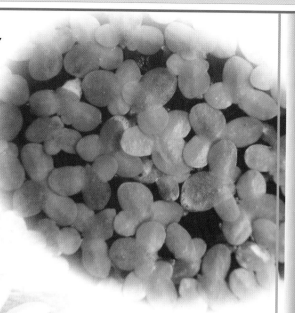

Most **Water Lilies** open for three days in succession, closing at night.

▼ **Aquatic plants** have a very thin cuticle or sometimes it is absent. The primary function of cuticles is to prevent water loss, thus most water plants have no need for cuticles.

Sea grass are monocots which live in the sea.

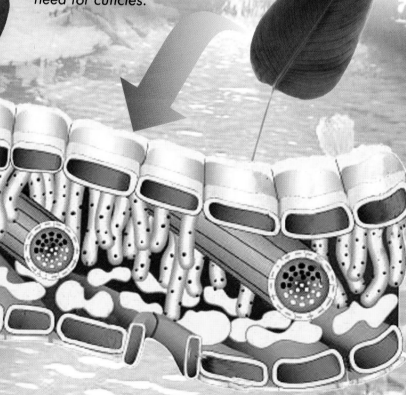

Hydrilla elongates rapidly to reach water surface and branches out at water surface, More light can be obtained at the water surface.

31

Desert Plants

Desert plants can grow in extreme dry conditions. Their stems are often swollen, and their leaves are spiny or waxy to avoid loss of water from leaves. Their strange appearance is a result of their remarkable adaptations to the challenges of the desert climate.

▼ *The **Saguaro Cactus** has a smooth and waxy stem and is covered with two-inch spines.*

▶ ***Triangle-leaf bursage** is a small, round shrub about 1 1/2 feet tall and 2 feet wide.*

▼ All **Cacti** are succulents that store water in fleshy leaves, stems or roots.

▶ The **Joshua Tree** grows in arid deserts; they often grow in groups called groves.

Desert plants often shed leaves during dry periods and enter a deep dormancy to reduce the loss of water through transpiration.

The brittlebush is a common plant of the Mojave and Sonoron deserts. It is a small deciduous shrub which grows as a low, roundish mound 2 to 5 feet high.

Alpine Plants

Alpine plants grow on mountains. Most Alpine plants can grow in sandy and rocky soil. Plants have also adapted to the dry conditions. There are only about 200 species of Alpine plants.

▶ The **Alpine Phacelia** blooms in mid-summer.

▼ The **Wild Potato** *is a relative of the cultivated potato, and is found in the alpine biome of the Andes Mountains.*

▼ **Moss Campion** *only grows about 5-15 cm tall, hugging the ground for warmth.*

▼ *The oldest known tree is **"Methuselah"**, Pristtecone, which is about 5,000 years old.*

Pygmy Bitterroot is only found in the mountains of western North America.

Bear Grass looks like a grass, but really belongs to the lily family. It is about 4.5 feet tall.

The plant shown in the picture is **Mountain Ash**.

Quiz time!

1. Wild potato is commonly found in?

2. Colour of map lichen is?

3. Bristlecone pine is found at an elevation of?

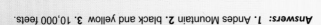

Answers: 1. Andes Mountain 2. black and yellow 3. 10,000 feets.

Ornamental Plants

An ornamental plant is grown for its ornamental qualities, rather than for its commercial or other value. Several dozens of ornamental plants grow as seasonal, annual or perennial herbs, shrubs, and trees. Most commonly they are grown for display of their flowers. Other common ornamental features include leaves, scent, fruit, stem and bark.

▲ The **Lily** family contains many beautiful plants and a number of these are edible.

◄ *Lavender is typically grown as an ornamental plant in gardens, but may also be grown as a crop plant for the production of lavender oil.*

▶ Chinese believe that a gift of living **bamboo** brings good fortune.

▶ **Canna indica**, often known as Indian Shot, looks somewhat like a banana plant. It adds an exotic air to the garden.

Violas are very common garden plants and are usually very easy to grow.

Bonsai are beautiful and graceful plants that reflect the patience and care of their owners.

Caladium is often known as elephant ear and is indigenous to Brazil.

Edible Plants

Fruits and vegetables are not only the parts of the plants that we eat. Apart from these, stems, leaves, seeds and roots are also eaten. There are also a few edible leaf stalks such as celery, as well as some edible flowers, such as broccoli and cauliflower.

▶ **Broccoli leaves** and cauliflower leaves are very similar, However, broccoli leaves tend to be blue-green in color compared to the bright green **cauliflower leaves**.

◀ **Turnips** and rutabagas are grown mainly for their enlarged roots. Turnips are easy to confuse with rutabaga, but rutabagas are larger and more yellow on the bottom.

▶ The part of the **carrot** plant that is eaten is the root. It is usually orange, elongated and pointed at the tip.

▶ All parts of the **onion** are edible but they are most often grown for their bulb, which is a modified stem.

▶ **Corn** grows in "ears," each of which is covered in rows of kernels that are then protected by the silk-like threads called "corn silk" and encased in a husk.

Basil leaves are used as a seasoning in both fresh and cooked dishes.

Celery is grown for its fibrous leaf stalks (petioles). The individual stalks can range from yellow-green to dark green.

The part of the potato plant we eat is called the tuber, which is actually an enlarged underground stem.

39

Medicinal Plants

A medicinal plant is used to prevent diseases. As many as 80% of the world's people rely for their primary health care on traditional medicines, most types of which use remedies made from plants.

◄ *Lavender* can be used in headache

Did you know?

Snakeroot is used in snakebites.

▶ **Garlic** is used in colds, fever, cough, bronchitis, high blood pressure, headache and rheumatism.

◀ **Yarrow** is an excellent treatment for colds, fever, indigestion, gastric inflammation and internal bleeding; expectorant and diaphoretic.

▼ **Cardamom** is used to treat infections in teeth and gums, to prevent and treat throat troubles.

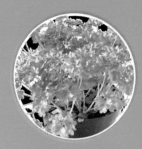

Parsley is used in kidney problems.

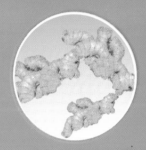

In Myanmar, **ginger** and local sweet which is made from palm tree juice are boiled together and taken to prevent the Flu.

Dried leaves of **Foxglove** contain glycosides and are used as powerful heart stimulant.

41

Carnivorous Plants

Carnivorous plants attract, capture and kill its prey. They digest and absorb the nutrients of its prey and this is what makes them carnivorous plants. Carnivorous plants usually grow in places where the soil is poor in nutrients, especially nitrogen.

▶ **Nepenthes** plants are native to Asia, Australia, The Philippines, Borneo, Malaysia, Sumatra, and some other Pacific islands.

◀ **Pitcher plant** is a carnivorous plant and is often found in nitrogen-starved bogs.

▶ Butterwort is a carnivorous plant. It produces a glandular fluid on the leaves to attract, catch, and digest small insects. The leaves will slightly curl so that the fluid will pool around its victim.

Venus flytrap is the most famous carnivorous plants. It occur naturally in swampy, marshy areas.

◀ **Octopus Plant** has the glue-tipped tentacles.

Bladderwort is a member of a fascinating group of freely-floating, rootless, carnivorous aquatic plants.

Waterwheel plant is a remarkable aquatic carnivorous plant.

Quiz time!

1. Most carnivorous plants are found in which kind of terrain?

2. Carnivores plants trap insects because they lack.........

3. Which plant is shown in the picture......

Answers: 1. Acidic Soil **2.** Nitrogen **3.** Darlingtonia californica

43

Parasitic Plants

A parasitic plant is one that derives some or all of its substance from another plant. Parasitic plants have a modified root, the haustorium, that penetrates the host plant and connects to the xylem, phloem, or both.

◄ **Dodders** are parasitic flowering plants. Its seed germinates in the ground and sends up a reddish filamentous curling stem which contact a suitable host.

► *Rafflesia is a parasitic plant that lacks roots, stems, and leaves.*

The parasitic method of nutrition is made possible by special structures called **haustoria.**

◀ **Mistletoe** thrives on the branches of a tree or shrub.

▶ **Yellow Rattle** is a semi-parasitic plant that gains its nutrients from the roots of neighboring plant.

Hydnora lack chlorophyll and must rely totally on the contents of the xylem and the phloem of the host.

Owl's clover obtains water and nutrients by connecting to the host xylem via the haustorium.

Quiz time!

1. A plant that cannot complete its life cycle without a host is called.........

2. A plant that completes its life cycle without depending on the host plant is called ....

Answers: 1. Obligate Parasite 2. Facultive Parasite

45

Plant Diseases

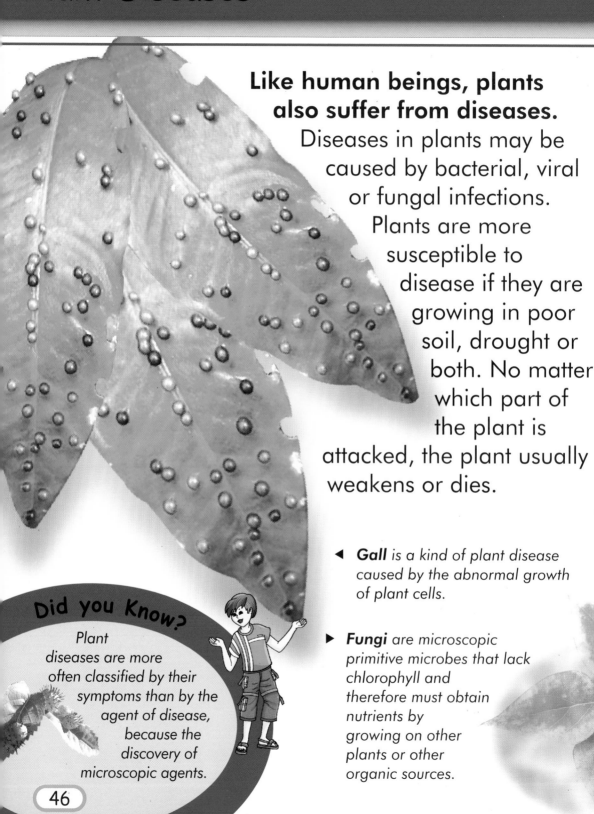

Like human beings, plants also suffer from diseases. Diseases in plants may be caused by bacterial, viral or fungal infections. Plants are more susceptible to disease if they are growing in poor soil, drought or both. No matter which part of the plant is attacked, the plant usually weakens or dies.

◄ **Gall** is a kind of plant disease caused by the abnormal growth of plant cells.

► **Fungi** are microscopic primitive microbes that lack chlorophyll and therefore must obtain nutrients by growing on other plants or other organic sources.

Did you Know?

Plant diseases are more often classified by their symptoms than by the agent of disease, because the discovery of microscopic agents.

◄ **Tobacco Mosaic Virus (TMV)** *is a kind of virus that infects plants, especially tobacco.*

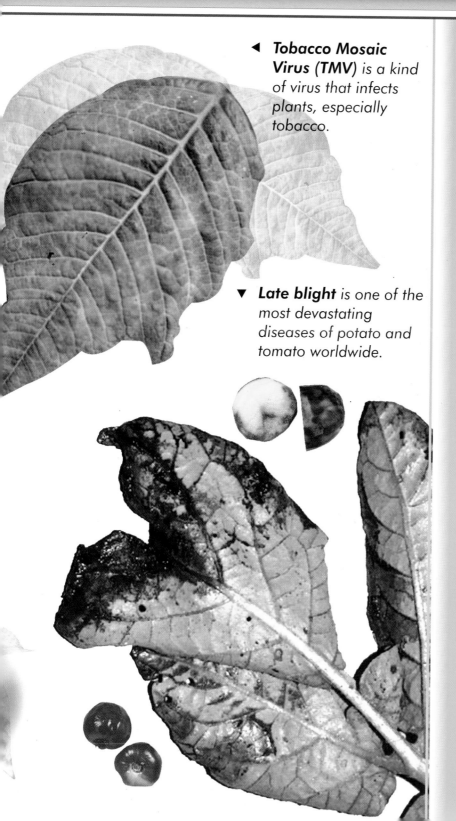

▼ **Late blight** *is one of the most devastating diseases of potato and tomato worldwide.*

Ergot of Rye *is a plant disease that is caused by the fungus named Claviceps purpurea.*

Clubroot *is one of the most common plant diseases occurring in cabbage and is caused by the soil-borne fungus Plasmodiophora brassicae.*

Glossary

Aspirin: A medicine that relieves pain and reduces fever.

Bark: The tough outer covering of the woody stems and roots of trees.

Biome: An ecosystem that covers a large geographic area where plants of one type live due to the specific climate in the area.

Bronchitis: Infection of the airways (bronchi) leading to the lungs.

Chlorophyll: The pigment in leaves that is responsible for trapping light energy from the sun.

Curl: A spiral or curved shape.

Dispersed: Scattered in different directions.

Elongated: Having more length than width.

Embryo: The early stages of development before an organism becomes self supporting.

Exotic: Intriguingly unusual or different.

Ferns: A vascular plant that does not produce seeds but reproduces by spores.

Fossils: Mineralized remains of life-forms of the past.

Harsh: Unpleasant or uncomfortable.

Herbs: Soft-stemmed, aromatic plants used fresh or dried to flavour dishes.

Germination: The first stage in the development of a plant from seed.

Husk: The outer cellulose covering of seeds and grains.

Inflammation: Inflammation is the first response of the immune system to infection or irritation.

Inflorescence: The mode of arrangement of the flowers of plants.

Mesozoic Era: This era contains the Triassic, Jurassic, and Cretaceous periods and marked by the appearance of birds, mammals, and flowering plants.

Monocots: The seeds of which have only one cotyledon.

Permian age: The last period of geologic time in the Paleozoic Era characterized by the formation of the supercontinent Pangaea and the rise of conifers.

Pigment: A substance that produces color in plant tissue.

Pollen sac: The microsporangium of a seed plant in which pollen is produced.

Rheumatism: Any painful disorder of the joints or muscles or connective tissues.

Rhizoids: Hair-like structures in the plants that serves as a root for bryophytes.

Shrub: A woody plant of relatively low height, having several stems arising from the base and lacking a single trunk.

Spores: The reproductive cells in plants that can grow into an new plants without male and female parts.

Stout: Hardy and rugged physical strength.

Tropical: An area where temperatures do not go below freezing point and it is warm enough to support plant growth all year long.

Vines: A weak-stemmed plant that derives its support from climbing, twining, or creeping along a surface.

DISCOVER THE WORLD

THE BIRDS

Birds are warm-blooded vertebrate animals that have wings, feathers, and beak. They have strong, hollow bones and powerful flight muscles. Birds also have a very strong heart, and an efficient way of breathing. There are about 9,000 species of birds, and all are grouped under the class Aves.

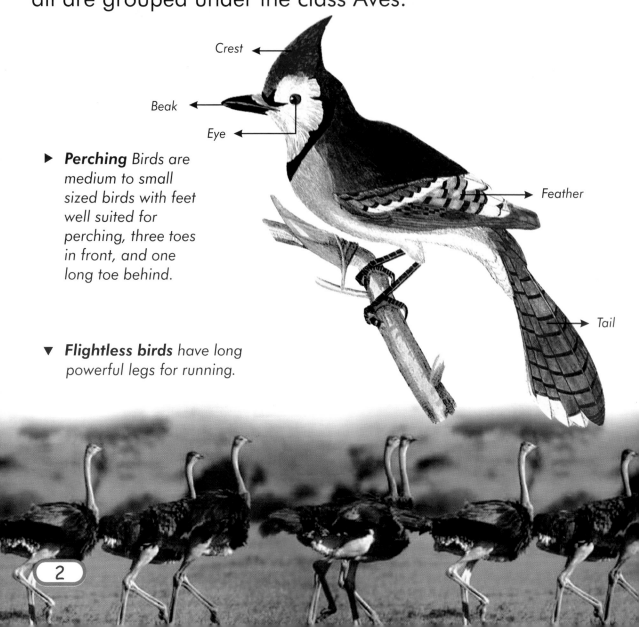

Crest

Beak

Eye

Feather

Tail

▶ **Perching** Birds are medium to small sized birds with feet well suited for perching, three toes in front, and one long toe behind.

▼ **Flightless birds** have long powerful legs for running.

2

◀ A bird uses its **beak** for feeding, and it is shaped according to what a bird eats. The bill is one of the characteristics used to identify birds.

Claws are prominent in birds of Prey like Eagles.

▶ **Swift Birds** are unable to perch but they can climb a vertical surface very well with their sharp small claws.

Birds that climb such as Woodpeckers and Parrots, have two toes forward and two backward.

Swimming Birds have webs of skin between the toes such as the Duck.

Quiz time!

1. Which is the only wingless bird in the world?

2. Which bird is known for its poisonous skin and feathers?

3. Which is the most common bird in the world?

Kiwi

Answers: 1. Kiwi! 2. Hooded Pitohui of Papua, New Guinea 3. Domestic chicken.

What Makes Birds Special ?

Birds are unique. Birds have two reasons for being special. First, all birds have feathers. And second, everything about a bird is fast. They breathe faster than any other animal. Their heart beats faster, and their body temperature is higher than any other animal in the vast animal kingdom.

▲ As birds are **warm blooded** therefore their body temperature remains the same even in differing temperatures.

◀ Birds eat **"high-octane"** foods which are high in calories, like seeds, nuts, fruits, fish, and rodents.

Eagle can glide and soar for hours.

▶ The **retina** of a bird's eye is 2 times as thick as a man's. A sparrow hawk can see 8 times more than human beings.

The **Great Bustard** is considered the biggest flying bird, in the world today .

Flight muscles have the biggest and strongest muscles which helps in flying.

Where Do Birds Live?

Birds are found everywhere from the poles to the equator and some birds have the ability to fly everywhere.

▶ **Penguins** are adapted to survive in the freezing climate of Antarctica.

▼ Lakes are often important bird habitat, and sometimes, millions of birds can be found nesting, resting, and feeding on them.

▶ **Goshawks** *make their nest in the dense forest.*

Bluebirds *prefer to live in open grassy areas near a park, golf course, meadow, pasture or even a cemetery.*

Flamingos *are found in the wetlands.*

◀ The **Cactus Wren** *lives in desert thickets, and areas with large cactus, like the Cholla. It needs areas with cactus or thorny plants or bushes strong enough to hold its large nests.*

Did you Know?

The **Gila Woodpecker** depends upon the Giant Saguaro as its home.

7

Birds Adaptation

Birds are warm-blooded vertebrate animals that have wings, feathers and a beak. Flying birds have strong, hollow bones, and powerful flight muscles. No other animals can travel faster than birds.

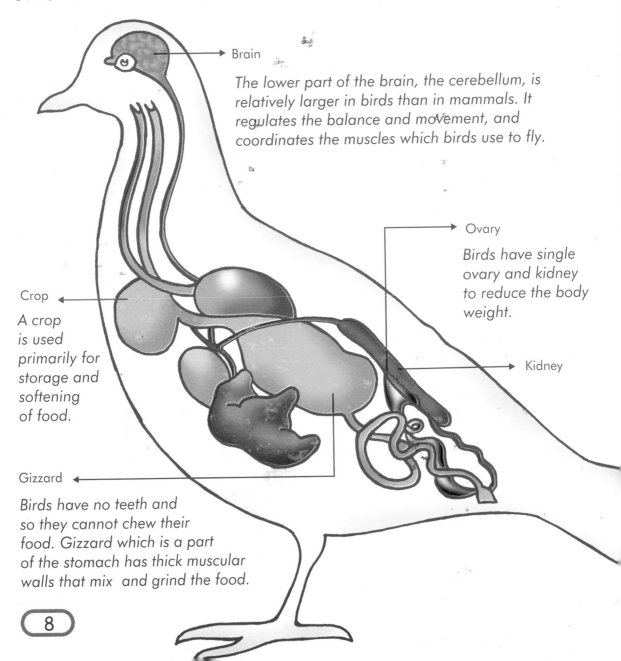

Brain

The lower part of the brain, the cerebellum, is relatively larger in birds than in mammals. It regulates the balance and movement, and coordinates the muscles which birds use to fly.

Ovary

Birds have single ovary and kidney to reduce the body weight.

Crop

A crop is used primarily for storage and softening of food.

Kidney

Gizzard

Birds have no teeth and so they cannot chew their food. Gizzard which is a part of the stomach has thick muscular walls that mix and grind the food.

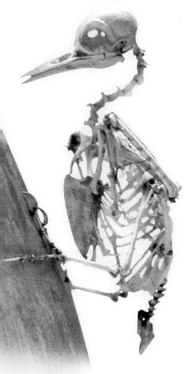

◀ Birds have **Pneumatic bones**. These bones are hollow from inside, which reduces the overall body weight, and helps the bird in flying.

Birds have four chambered **heart,** and are warmed blooded like mammals.

Air Sac

Birds have thin-walled pouches called air sacs. The sacs are connected to the lungs. These air sacs help the birds for cooling down since they are unable to sweat.

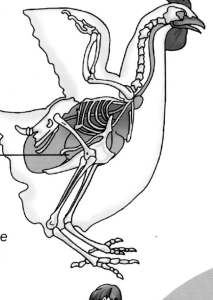

Sternum is well developed in birds. All the flight muscles are attached to the sternum, also called the breast bone.

Did you know?

Feathers are highly modified scales. Apart from flying, a feather also helps in thermal insulation and courtship.

Birds Nest

Birds' nests are necessary during the breeding seasons for the proper development of a bird's eggs. Nest size, shape, and building materials vary greatly among birds. Nest placement and design, along with the behaviour of the parents and young; combine to provide protection from temperature extremes and predators.

▲ **Barn Swallow** are famous for building their nest anywhere. Typical nesting habitats are burn, bridge, culvert, and other artificial structure. They nest in colonies.

◄ **Bald faced Hornets** make those large, almost round nests. You can see in trees after the leaves have fallen in winter.

▼ **Woodpeckers** excavate their nests in tree trunks or branches. These nest cavities offer safety from predators and a comfortable micro climate for the eggs and the young ones.

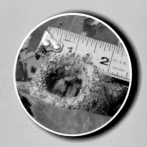

Hummingbird builds the smallest nest measuring about 1sq cm.

The **Australian Honeyeater** sometimes filches the thick fur to line its nest.

Coot Bird builds nest of dead reeds and grasses near water's edge or on water.

11

Bird Eggs

All birds lay eggs but some lay them in nest. The eggs are quickly formed inside the female bird's body and laid. The eggs are then incubated outside the body. The outer shell of eggs are made up of calcium carbonate that protects the developing chicks. Eggs have inside them everything that a baby bird needs to grow to the point of being ready to be hatched.

◀ **Robin** *is the only bird that lays* **blue coloured eggs.**

▶ **West Indian vervain Hummingbird** *at 10 mm (0.39" in) in length and 0.375gm in weight has the* **smallest egg.**

Embryo

After hatching, the embryo develops into a new young one.

Albumin

The albumin is not only the embryo's water supply, but also assists the movement of gases from the embryo to the shell as well as provides some shock protection.

Yolk

The yolk is a fatty food store for the developing embryo.

Owl's eggs *are known for its round shape among all the birds' eggs.*

The **Maleo Bird** *has a record for the longest interval between eggs laying, which is 1012 days.*

▲ The extinct giant **Elephant Bird** of Madagascar laid eggs as big in volume as seven Ostrich eggs and bigger than any Dinosaur egg.

Did you Know?

The **Ostrich** lays the **heaviest egg**, each is about six inches long and weighs up to 2½ pounds.

13

Parenthood in Birds

All birds show parental care of their young for the first few days. Because the chicks are born helpless. The parents protect and feed their offspring, until the young have learned to look after themselves.

▶ **Grebes** *carry their young ones on their backs.*

▼ **American Goldfinch** *feeds through its beak to its chicks during the initial stages of development.*

▼ A female **Mallard** with a **Duckling Mallard.**

Incubation is common in birds during which they provide heat to the eggs by sitting on

▼ The male **Great Reed Warbler** may have several females nesting in its territory, but only the lucky "primary" female whose eggs hatch first get his help in rearing her young!

Murrelet Chicks are the most independent at the time of birth.

Did you Know?

The female **Hornbill** seals herself into the nest, and stays inside the tree cavity throughout incubation, leaving only a tiny hole.

15

Birds Language

Birds have their own ways of communication known as bird language. Birds communicate through variety of ways. They use their body parts and voices to express their wide range of emotions. Without proper communication birds would starve, loose their way during migration, be unable to defend their territory or find a mate.

▼ If a bird is **flipping** its **wings**, it means it has lost its balance and is trying to correct itself.

◀ **Cockatoos** tap their feet as a sign of dominance over their territory. This usually only happens when they feel their territory is threatened.

Head bobbing is a common sign that they do when they are hungry and want to be fed.

Growling is common in birds to show aggressivenes.

▼ **Fainning of tail** feathers shows birds aggressive behaviour.

Did you Know?

Rapid **"clicking"** of the tongue against the beak means "I want to be friendly, I won't hurt you". This invitational behavior is most often seen among parrots.

17

Birds Songs

Birds' songs are the voices that birds make, and are very melodious. A bird song has two main functions: to defend a territory, and to attract a mate. Male birds do these things, so, throughout the bird world, it is usually the males singing the songs.

▶ The **Kakapo** has one of the most far-carrying songs of any bird. He may boom all night for three months to attract females in the area to his display court. Its sound can be heard as much as three miles away.

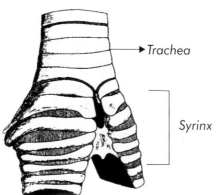

Trachea

Syrinx

◀ The birds produce sound through organ **syrinx**, which is equivalent to human sound box. The syrinx contains membranes which vibrate and generate sound waves when air from the lungs is passed over them.

The Brown Thrasher can produce more than 2000 songs in its repertoire.

▶ The **red-winged Blackbird** female sings two distinct types of songs during the breeding season.

The Sedge Warbler produces some of the longest and most complicated of all bird songs.

▼ **Magpie-larks** sing a duet to defend their territory in the Australian bush. One bird utters a loud metallic "tee-hee" that is immediately followed by the other's "pee-o-wee, pee-o-wit".

Did you Know?

White-browed Sparrow Weavers sing group choruses, which they use to defend their territories.

19

Birds Mating

A bird without a mate is a bird without offspring. The sequence and variety of courting behaviours vary widely among birds. Mating begin with territorial defence and song followed by mate-attraction displays, courtship feeding, and selection of a nest site.

▶ *Geese, Swans* and *Eagles* are known for having only one mate until one of them dies.

◀ *Gambel's quail* sometimes leave young with the male, and seek another brood with a new father. In order to entice females, males offer small bits of food during feeding.

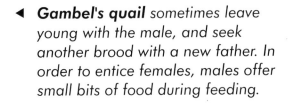

▶ *Ducks* usually look for a mate in winter. The males attracts the females with their colourful plumage or feathers. The females then lead the males to their breeding ground in spring.

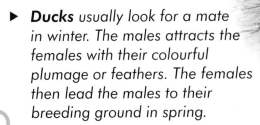

The **Superb Fairy Wren** of Southern Australia is the most promiscuous bird in the world. Both males and females have multiple partners.

▲ **Kingfisher** is by nature a solitary bird. However, during the mating and nesting season, they pair off just like other birds.

A male **Tern** starts his courtship by bringing the female a small fish, held crosswise in his beak.

▼ After **Hummingbirds** mate, the male court and mate with another female. Females raise the babies alone.

Did you Know?

House Wrens builds multiple nests, and let the female choose the one she prefers.

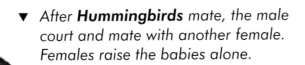

Birds Migration

Migration is the seasonal movement of birds for purpose of food, reproduction or to avoid harsh weather be it warm or winter. Before migration, birds eat more food, which is stored as fat for their long journey. Fat is normally 3% to 5% of the bird's mass. Some migrants almost double their body weights by storing fat before migration.

▼ Some migrating birds leave their home and fly when the seasons change and for this, the birds use the **position of the sun** during the day to navigate.

▼ The **Arctic Tern** may hold the record for the longest migration, since it flies about 30,000 km (18,600 miles) each year travelling between its Arctic breeding ground and the non-breeding area in the Antarctic.

◄ In still air, most **Songbirds** fly at 20 to 30 mph. Waterfowls and Shorebirds can fly at 30 to 50 mph. A tailwind allows the bird to fly faster.

Magnetic mineral magnetite just above the nostril help birds to find out north and south directions.

▼ **Waterfowls** are presently the most prominent and economically important group of migratory birds of the North American continent.

The Ruby-throated Hummingbird weighs only 4.8 grams and can use stored fat to fuel a non-stop, 24-hour flight.

Did you Know?

Bar-headed Geese have been recorded as high as 29,000 feetwhen they migrate over the Himalayas.

Importance of Birds

Birds eat insects and control pests in gardens and farms. They aid in the pollinisation of plants. Birds also have a good system for spreading seeds.
Birds are also raised for meat and eggs.
Humans also have a long history of keeping birds like parrots as pets.

▶ *Parrots* *are particularly popular as they can be trained to imitate human speech and even to whistle.*

◀ *Robins and Sparrows, are highly effective against cabbageworms, tomato worms, and leaf beetles.*

▶ One **Bobwhite** may rid a field of as many as 15,000 weeds a day.

▼ Over the centuries, the droppings of **Ocean Birds** have formed huge deposits in certain areas of the world. This waste matter, which is called guano, makes excellent fertilizer. The mining of guano for fertilizer is an important industry in Peru and the small Pacific island nation of Nauru.

Hummingbirds pollinate certain flowers that produce nectar. In fact, this helps in pollination of flowers and acclerates seed germination.

Rats and mice can cause huge losses on farms by eating stored grain. **Hawks** and **owls** prey on these animals.

Did you Know?

Birds tell us about the world's biodiversity. Birds are useful environmental indicators, helping us to locate important places and alerting us to environmental change.

25

Intelligent Birds

Birds are believed to be more intelligent than reptiles. Many birds are as intelligent as mammals of comparable size. The level of intelligence among birds may vary.

▲ **Green-backed Herons** from around the world use bread and insects as bait to catch fish.

▲ **The Clarke's Nutcracker**, a North American crow, collects up to 30,000 pine seeds over three weeks in November, then carefully buries them for safe keeping over an area of 200 square miles. Over the next eight months, it succeeds in retrieving over 90 percent of them, even when they are covered in snow.

▼ **The Woodpecker Finch**, a bird of the Galapagos, is another consummate toolmaker. It snaps off a twig, trim it to size and use it to pry insects out of bark.

New Caledonian Crows have been observed in the wild to use stick tools with their beaks to extract insects from logs.

The **African Grey Parrot** is a bird believed to have the intelligence and emotional make-up of a 3 to 4-year old child.

◄ Another example of birds' intelligence is **anting**, where they pick up an ant and rub it through their feathers or even sit on ants. It is thought that the formic acid from ants works as a repellent for fleas and lice.

Did you Know?

Blue Tits are commonly found opening the tin foiled bottle caps in order to feed on the cream.

Birds of Paradise

Birds of paradise is the most amazing and incredibly colourful family of birds. Male birds of paradise are more colourful and attractive than females. They are commonly found in New Guinea and adjacent islands.

▶ The **Male Greater** bird of paradise has long, yellow flank plumes, brown back and wings, green throat, a black breast and can be up to 18 inches long.

◀ **Cardinal** is a bird common in North America. It is sometimes called Redbird. It has a crest of feathers on its head that can be raised to threaten an enemy.

Chickadee is a small bird from North America measuring 4 to 6 inches in length.

◄ **Bluebird** is North American birds known for their brilliant, blue feathers.

Wood Thrush has bright cinnamon-coloured upper parts, and spotted white breast and sides.

◄ **Finch** is famous for its red colour.

Barn Swallow is well-known for its blue colour. It is the national bird of Estonia.

Quiz time!

1. What is unique about the Bird of Paradise?

2. To which family does the Bird of Paradise belong?

3. How many species of Birds of Paradise exist today?

4. Which bird has been shown in the image?

Answers: 1. Plumage **2.** Paradisaeidae **3.** 32 species **4.** Riflebird

29

Flightless Birds

Not all birds can fly, but they all have feathers.
Birds that cannot fly are known as flightless birds, and
are grouped under ratites. Flightless birds evolved
from flying birds.

◄ The **Emperor Penguin** is the
largest penguin. It cannot fly,
but it swims very well, and spend
most of their lives in the sea.

▶ **The Emu** is the third largest flightless bird in the world and second in the Australia. It can swim very well, also run upto 30 m/h (50 km/h).

▼ The **Common Rhea** is a large, flightless bird from the forests of South America. It is a fast runner; when it does, its neck is almost horizontal to the ground.

The smallest flightless bird is the inaccessible **Island Rail** measuring 12.5 cm in length.

The **tiny Stephens Island Wren** was the only flightless and the smallest songbird in the world.

Did you Know?

The **Cassowary** is the largest flightless bird in Australia and the second biggest bird in the world.

Fowl Birds

Fowls are any one of several kinds of large birds that nest on the ground. Most domestic fowls can fly only short distances. Over the years, people have domesticated certain wild fowls. This discovery led to the development of poultry—i.e., domesticated fowl that farmers raise for meat and eggs. Chickens are probably the oldest kinds of poultry.

◀ *Tragopan is the name of five species of quail like birds. They live in forests high on mountain slopes of southern and central Asia. Males have a bright-coloured lappet on the throat, and a pair of blue, fleshy, erectile horns on each side of the head.*

◄ **Peacock** is one of the showiest of all birds because of its great size and the beauty of its feathers. The word, peacock refers only to the male peafowl. The female bird is called a peahen. However, most people use the term, peacock for both female and male.

Nene the official bird of Hawaii also known as Hawaiian goose, is a rare bird of Hawaii.

Curassow is the name of a group of large birds that live in the forests of tropical America. It has a crest of feathers on top of the head.

Ptarmigan is the name of a group of birds that live in northern parts of the northern hemisphere, such as Alaska, the Aleutian ◄ Islands, and Greenland.

Did you Know?

Turkey is a large North American bird. Male turkeys are called toms, and femaleturkeys are known as hens.

33

Water Birds

Water Birds are wonderfully adapted to their aquatic lives. Their feet function as paddles, and their feathers are constructed to be waterproof and air tight. Water birds teach their children how to swim and where to find food.

▶ **Great Frigatebirds** are large seabirds with long pointed wings and long forked tails.

◀ **Ducks** have webbed feet, designed for swimming. Male ducks are called "Drakes," and females are called "Hens." They can live from 2-12 years, depending on species.

▼ The great **Cormorant** is reputed to be a good fish catcher.

▼ **Boobies** are strictly marine birds which live primarily in warm waters, feeding on fish. They come ashore only to nest or roost.

Loon is a fish-eating bird with a short tail, webbed feet, and a laugh like cry.

The pouch of a **pelican** has a capacity to carry 12 quarts.

Did you Know?

Albatrosses has long, narrow wings that enable them to glide for thousands of miles without flapping their wings.

Nocturnal Birds

Those birds that are active at night are called Nocturnal birds. These birds have large eyes that enable them to see better in dim light. They also have slightly larger ears that helps them to hear the prey better in dark.

◄ **Owls** have the best hearing of all birds. Their ears are located on the sides of their heads, and are hidden by feathers.

◄ **The Herons, the Jungle Crow, Carrion Crow, Gray Starling,** and the **White Wagtail** sleep In large groups easily spotted by many people.

The prey of a **Yellow-crowned Night Heron** normally consists of fish, frogs, grasshoppers, and occasionally snakes, but its primary diet is crustaceans.

▶ *Kakapo* is an owl like flightless New Zealand Parrot. They alive at night.

◄ **Ruffed Grouse** do much of their drumming at night.

Kiwi has a good sense of smell.

Did you Know?

Carri on Crow is one of the cleverest, and most adaptable of all night birds.

37

Birds of Snow

Birds which are found in extreme cold climate such as the Arctic and the Antarctic regions are known as the 'birds of snow'. Cold climate is not a big problem for these birds for they are equipped with several layers of fluffy and insulating feathers on their body to trap the heat.

▶ **Antarctic Fulmars** *are readily identified by their pale silver-grey plumage, white head and black-tipped flight feathers.*

▶ **The Ptarmigan** *is completely covered with feathers including its beak and the feet. It is the feathers on the feet that make it able to walk on soft snow without sinking.*

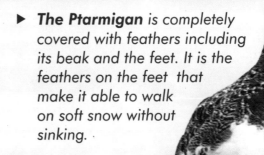

◀ **Penguins** *live in the Antarctic and the Arctic circles, and have a thick layer of fat under their skin to protect them from cold.*

▶ **Ravens** are able to survive the cold because their black feathers absorb heat.

The South Polar **Skua** is recognised as the world's most southerly bird.

Large colonies of **Snow Geese** nest by the Tundra pools. The nests are built of moss and other Tundra plants.

▲ **Gyrfalcons** are the most northerly of the Falcons, making their homes in Arctic Europe, Asia, North America and Greenland.

▶ **Puffins** are sea birds that can fly, swim, and dig burrows.

Cormorants are excellent divers with a recorded maximum dive of 400 feet.

Champion Birds

The birds enduring the harshest conditions are called the Champion Birds. Living higher, flying faster, and diving deeper, certainly gives these bird, an edge over their competitors.

◄ **Crossbill** is the only bird capable of moving its beak in two directions, allowing it to break open the immensely tough ponderosa pine.

► The **Flamingo** is another candidate for a bird which reside in the hot, shallow soda lakes and salt lagoons of Africa, where the water is salty and unpleasant and the Temperatures can reach up to 60°C.

Did you Know?

The **Woodcock** is one of the best camouflaged of all birds. A Sand Grouse could be described as the busiest eater in the bird world.

▶ The bird with the keenest sense of smell may be the **Turkey Vulture**. It can detect a meat from half a mile away.

▼ **Arctic Tern** is the longest distance flying bird that could fly 11,ooo miles away towards the atlantica during the breeding season.

The Antarctic Penguins dive to over 1,300 feet, with a speed of nine miles per hour.

Great Gray Owl, hunts entirely by sound with its extraordinary super-stereo hearing.

Albatrosses are the longest-lived birds that can glide for hours without flapping their wings.

41

Endangered Birds

Endangered birds are those birds that exist today, but are on the verge of extinction. The number of these birds are very less due to the increasing number of predators or the changing environmental conditions.

▶ The **Gouldian Finch** is an endangered species due to the fact that it only exists in a single population, and that a continuing decline is projected in the number of mature adults.

◀ Today the crested **Shelduck** is classified as a critically endangered species due to an estimated population of less than 50 mature crested birds.

▶ The **California Condor** can be found in the United States. It is classified as a critically endangered species due to an estimated population of less than 50 mature individuals.

Long Beak Vulture is counted under the endangered species due to its low population.

Only 2500 species of **White-winged Duck** is alive today.

▶ **Siberian Crane**s are the third rarest of all cranes, and arguably the most endangered, with only about 3,000 known to exist in the world.

Did you Know?

Lear's Macaw species is seriously endangered because it has an extremely small population which breeds in one area, and is continuing to decline, principally as a result of trapping for trade.

Birds of Prey

Birds of prey are commonly known as raptors. They are meat eaters and use their feet, instead of their beak, to capture prey. They have exceptionally good vision, a sharp, hooked beak, and powerful feet with curved, sharp talons. There are about 500 species of birds of prey and they vary greatly in size.

▶ *Falcon is diurnal bird of prey. Its power drive may reach a velocity of about 180 kilometers per hour, the fastest of all birds.*

Did you Know?

In their hunting "dive" or "swoop," a **Peregrine Falcon** reaches a speed in excess of 200 miles per hour!

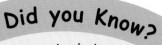

◀ *Eagles normally eat fish. They have long sharp beaks and curved talons to help hold the prey. They can fly with 8 pounds of food.*

Male Andean Condor with an 11-foot wingspan is the largest raptor.

▲ Of all an **Owl's** features, the most striking is its eyes which may account for one to five percent of the Owl's body weight, depending on the species. The forward facing aspect of the eyes give an Owl a wide range of "binocular" vision.

The Raven is the largest species of songbird and also all-black bird in the world.

Quiz time!

1. What are the claws of a bird of prey called?

2. Which Parrot is active at night?

3. What does a Toucan eat?

4. Which bird is shown in the picture?

Answers: 1. Talons 2. Kakap 3. Fruits and berries 4. Vulture

The 5-inch **Elf Owl** is the smallest birds of prey.

Dangerous Birds

Some birds which cause serious harm to human beings are known as dangerous birds. Also they are harmful when they eat crops and kill small pet animals.

▶ **Seagulls** are extremely aggressive, and are known to attack and even peck at people's heads to protect their nests and young ones.

◀ **The Rhea**, native to South America, is a large, flightless bird that can grow up to 60-80 pounds. They have heavily muscled legs, hard spurs on their feet, and their kicks can bring a force of 800 pounds per square inch.

▼ **Cassowaries** eat fungi, snails, insects, frogs, snakes and other small animals. They have also been observed to attack humans, though this usually is for self-defence.

Hawks pose serious dangers to humans, even if the birds are just babies.

▼ The only known poisonous bird in the world is **The Hooded Pitohui** of Papua, New Guinea. The poison is found in its skin and feathers.

Canada Geese are very aggressive. They may chase you away, and even bite you.

Did you Know?

Eagles are strong enough to carry away something that weighs even four pounds.

47

Glossary

Adaptable: Organizations that are able to respond quickly to external change.

Albumin: A protein found in egg white.

Binocular vision: Vision as a result of both eyes working as a team; when both eyes work together smoothly, accurately, equally and simultaneously.

Breeding: Production of animals or plants by inbreeding or hybridization.

Claws: A claw is a curved pointed growth found at the end of a toe or finger.

Courtship: The process of selecting and attracting a mate for sexual reproduction.

Diurnal: Animal active at day.

Egg Shell: The hard, calcium shell, secreted by a bird's shell gland, that surrounds and protects its eggs.

Eggs: Oval reproductive body of a female bird.

Embryo: An animal in its earliest stage of development.

Endangered: Animals whose life is in danger.

Flapping: The up and down motion of the wings.

Flightless Birds: Birds that can not fly.

Hooded: A hawk or other bird of prey when borne with a hood over its head.

Hooked: Curved down like an eagle's beak.

Insects: Invertebrate animals of the class Insecta.

Naturalist: A person who studies nature.

Nostril: Either one of the two external openings to the nasal cavity in the nose.

Plumage: The feathers of a bird.

Predators: Animals that hunt and kill other animals for food.

Prey: Animal hunted or caught for food.

Promiscuous: A mating behavior in which the male and female do not form lasting pair bonds; one male may mate with several females, or one female with several males.

Raptors: Carnivorous bird species (eg, owls, hawks, falcons) that prey on other birds, amphibians, reptiles, and mammals.

Repertoire: The complete vocal abilities of a bird, including its callnotes and songs.

Species: A classification of related organisms that can freely interbreed.

Syrinx: Organ of voice production in birds.

Talons: Sharply hooked claws on the foot of a meat eating birds.

Thermal insulation: Material used to reduce heat flow.

Vertebrate: An animal that has a backbone.

Wingspan: The distance between the tips of opposite wings.

Yolk: Inner part of an egg.